CITYSPOTS
REYK

Ethel Davies

Written and photographed by Ethel Davies
Front cover photograph copyright Alamy Images

Produced by 183 Books
Design/layout/maps: Chris Lane and Lee Biggadike
Editorial/project management: Stephen York

Published by Thomas Cook Publishing
A division of Thomas Cook Tour Operations Limited
PO Box 227, Units 15/16, Coningsby Road
Peterborough PE3 8SB, United Kingdom
email: books@thomascook.com
www.thomascookpublishing.com
+44 (0) 1733 416477

First edition © 2006 Thomas Cook Publishing
Text © 2006 Thomas Cook Publishing
Maps © 2006 Thomas Cook Publishing
ISBN-13: 978-1-84157-549-0
ISBN-10: 1-84157-549-6
Project Editor: Kelly Anne Pipes
Production/DTP: Steven Collins

Printed and bound in Spain by GraphyCems

CONTENTS

SYMBOLS & ABBREVIATIONS

The following symbols are used throughout this book:

☎ telephone   **🖷** fax   **✉** email   **🅦** website address
🅐 address   **🕒** opening times   **🅝** public transport connections

The following symbols are used on the maps:
🄸   Tourist Information Office
✈   Airport

Hotels and restaurants are graded by approximate price as follows:
£ budget price   **££** mid-range price   **£££** expensive
The local currency is the Kronur (see page 144)

24-HOUR CLOCK

All times in this book are given in the 24-hour clock system used widely in Europe and in most international transport timetables.

◑ *Contrasting old and new church spires dominate the city's skyline*

INTRODUCING
Reykjavik

Introduction

Bleakly beautiful, with cool breezes tempered by heat rising up from the land, modern yet still in touch with its Viking past, Reykjavik is a series of surprises.

The capital of Iceland is located on a relatively recently formed bay shaped by a glacier, where new buildings spring up along its shores. Small, with a population of barely more than half the entire country's 295,000, every amenity (and most western European shops) appear on the city's streets. Incredibly clean, energy springs from natural sources, with electricity generated by rushing rivers and glacial meltwater, and heat harnessed from geothermal forces within the earth.

With a strong Nordic heritage that can be traced back to individual Vikings from Norway, Icelandic words have barely changed from the language spoken by those first settlers, yet everyone also speaks English. The country is young, both physically, with active volcanoes still creating land, and administratively, with the establishment of independence from Denmark occurring in only 1944.

Residents of the capital city live well. The country as a whole is extremely affluent, with a very high standard of living and one of the longest life expectancies in the world. Most of the wealth stems from the fishing industry, with export of dried fish (salt cod) almost as important as fresh. Energy production and tourism are also money earners. With all this cash about, Reykjavikingurs like to spend it on things. The central city is full of fine crafts shops and art galleries, as well as both off-the-peg and custom design fashion venues. Bookshops are everywhere, selling photographic publications extolling the beauties of the country, as well as international newspapers and more usual goods. In the suburbs, huge malls offer even more shopping possibilities. Restaurants, though pricey, are excellent, with a huge range of eating houses offering both domestic and international cuisine.

Culturally, Reykjavik has some first-rate museums, particularly relating to the history and fine art of the nation. Even though a small country, Iceland has its performing arts well represented. The main houses of the National Opera, Symphony and Theatre are all in the capital. Smaller and more off-the-cuff theatre groups pop up in various venues, and the legendary music scene uses the city's clubs and pubs as its exploratory workshops.

The city has a well-deserved reputation for being a party town. Cafés, clubs, pubs and restaurants stay open so far into the night as to be the next morning. Weekend closing hours are officially five or six am, although places remain buzzing until the party is over. The action doesn't start till late, perhaps midnight, as people often like to have time to dress up for the occasion. Another reason for the delayed festivities is the high price of alcohol, a deliberate taxation effort on the part of the government to reduce alcoholism. This preventive measure doesn't stop the fun entirely, as even though the nightlife is primarily social, the proceedings can get pretty rowdy at times!

Visiting Reykjavik barely scratches the surface of seeing Iceland, and it's extremely easy to view the country's extraordinary landscape by taking day trips from the capital. Beaches, geysers, glaciers, lakes, mountains, volcanic landscapes and waterfalls are all easily accessible. Organised tours are readily available from hotels and guesthouses, car hire is simple, and driving is generally safe.

When to go

Reykjavik literally lights up in the summer as its location, just below the Arctic Circle, means it never gets dark. This time of year is the most popular for visitors, as the temperatures are reasonable and the daylight virtually endless. Costs of hotels reflect this preference, and summer is the more expensive option in a two-season pricing system. Some accommodation is available only during the months of June–September.

Alternatively, the winter, with its long nights, means that the aurora borealis, the spectacular Northern Lights show, is visible most evenings. Skiing is popular, especially in the north of the country, and sometimes even just outside Reykjavik. Festivals occur all year round, whether celebrating the arts, the changing of the seasons or simply just having a good time.

SEASONS & CLIMATE

Although it has the northern-most capital city in the world, Iceland is not as cold as the name implies. Surrounded by the Gulf Stream, a warm ocean current that comes from Florida, the climate is moderate all year long, being slightly warmer in the summer and a little colder in the winter.

Averages for Reykjavik are just below freezing in January and a little above 10°C (50°F) in the summer. Thermometers regularly record figures into the 20's C (70's F) during the warmer months, and T-shirt weather is not uncommon. At the colder periods of the year, temperatures throughout the country vary more widely, and the further north one goes the colder it gets.

● *The summertime marathons bring the crowds out in force*

ANNUAL EVENTS

Reykjavik has events happening all year round. Celebrations are often planned for adjacent weekends, so that dates are not fixed from year to year. Check with the tourist office or  www.tourinfo.is for a more complete list and more precise times.

January/February

Winter Festival Take a chance and indulge in some of the country's weirder more-or-less edible delicacies, including the legendary *Hákarl*, the inedible rotted shark meat.

Winter Lights Festival Creating a glow in the darkness, this event promotes art projects focusing on the themes of light and energy.

Food and Fun Here's an opportunity to taste gourmet cuisine, with the best of Iceland's chefs competing with their foreign counterparts.

March/April

Bun Day and Bursting Tuesday Just before Lent is Iceland's version of
Mardi Gras. The former encourages participants to stuff their faces
with cream buns, and the latter with more substantial fare (salted
meat and mushy peas).

First Day of Summer Parades and street entertainment celebrate
the arrival of the (Icelandic) summer season.

May/June

Reykjavik Art Festival (12 May–2 June 2006) One of Iceland's most
important cultural festivals, this event has been held since 1970, and
brings together the best in local and international visual and
performing arts.

Festival of the Sea Parades, arts, crafts, food and sailing
competitions commemorate the old Icelandic Seamen's Day.

Icelandic National Day – 17 June This is a giant street party in
honour of the granting of Independence from Denmark, in 1944,
lasting all the very long day, due to the midnight sun.

The Arctic Open In Akureyri, Iceland's second city, this golf
tournament on midsummer's day is the best known of the midnight
sun competitions.

July/August

Gay Pride Rapidly becoming a tradition, this flamboyant festival
draws people from all over the world.

Culture Night and Marathon Virtually every gallery, museum,
restaurant, shop and business in Reykjavik opens its doors,
presenting free displays and performances. Beginning with several
mid-morning marathons of different lengths, the day ends at
midnight with a massive firework display.

September/October

As the summer comes to an end, there are several arts festivals, including: the Dance festival, Tango festival, The Reykjavík International Literature Festival, Reykjavik International Film Festival and Reykjavík Jazz Festival.

Iceland Airwaves This rock and pop event takes place at various venues, including the Blue Lagoon (see page 106).

November/December

31 December The firework display is legendary at this fantastic New Year's Eve celebration in a great party town.

PUBLIC HOLIDAYS
New Year's Day 1 Jan
Maundy Thursday 13 Apr 2006, 5 Apr 2007
Good Friday 14 Apr 2006, 6 Apr 2007
Easter Sunday 17 Apr 2006, 9 Apr 2007
Easter Monday 18 Apr 2006, 10 Apr 2007
May Day 1 May
Ascension Day 25 May 2006, 17 May 2007
Whit Sunday 4 June 2006, 27 May 2007
Whit Monday 5 June 2006, 28 May 2007
National Day 17 June
Summer Bank Holiday 7 Aug 2006, 6 Aug 2007
Christmas Eve 24 Dec, public holiday from noon
Christmas Day 25 Dec
Boxing Day 26 Dec
New Year's Eve 31 Dec, public holiday from noon

Björk

The most famous Icelander, arguably even since the medieval writer of the sagas, Björk (meaning birch) has become an important figure in the rock and pop world. Never afraid to experiment or to reinvent herself, the Reykjavik-born singer and performance artist emerged from the city's rich but somewhat insular musical heritage. She has established herself as one of the most individual yet recognisable exponents of pop music.

Born Björk Gudmundsdóttir, but now identified just by her first name, the singer became well known as one of the leads in the Icelandic group, the Sugar Cubes. Popular in Iceland, but also with a cult following in the UK and the USA, the band formed in 1986, reaching its peak in 1988 with their first album, *Life's Too Good*. Björk was highly visible as the face of the band. In 1990, the members

⬤ *Reykjavik's most famous export has had success around the world*

began to pursue their own musical interests. Following the release of *Stick Around for Joy*, and despite the album's launch in Europe, the group disbanded in 1992. Björk then relaunched her career as a solo artist. Although having been involved in music since she was a child, and even having had solo (Icelandic) music success when she was 11, this time her first album, *Debut,* became a smash hit. With sales of over 3 million copies worldwide, the 1993 production established Björk as an independent musical force.

Her second album, *Post*, followed in 1995. Leaving her then home in the United Kingdom for Spain, she produced her third album, *Homogenic*, in 1997. At this point, the film director Lars von Trier saw her in her music video *It's All So Quiet*, and decided she would be the ideal star for his film *Dancer in the Dark* (2000). The awarding of the Best Actress Prize at Cannes confirmed his choice, but Björk decided she would not act again, as she considered herself a musician rather than an actress.

In 2002, Björk released her *Greatest Hits*, but the final choice of tracks on the album had been decided via the internet. It was up to her web-voting fans to determine which songs were the best or the most indicative of her career.

One of Björk's most widely seen appearances was at the August 2004 summer Olympics in Athens, Greece. There she sang her own *Oceania* (from the album, *Medúlla*). Ever the peformance artist, while she sang her dress unfurled into a huge map of the world, slowly covering the Olympic athletes.

Reykjavik's best known daughter continues to work, although perhaps in a more low-key fashion than before. Björk has recently moved into writing movie soundtracks and has just completed one for the film *Drawing Restraint 9*, directed by her boyfriend Matthew Barney. For further information visit Ⓦ www.bjork.com.

History

The story of the early history of the discovery of Iceland stems from traditional accounts, beginning with the Vikings in the 9th century . Naoddoddur apparently lost his way while sailing to the Faeroe Islands and found himself in an unknown country, which he named Snowland. He didn't remain there for long, and neither did the Swede Gardar Svavarsson, who circumnavigated Iceland in 860, and spent the darker months at today's Husavik. A Norwegian contemporary, Flóki Vilgerdarsson, came to the place with the intent of settling there, but the winter killed his livestock. He returned to his original home with tales of ice, and a new name for the country, Island (Iceland).

The medieval *Book of Settlements* continues the story, with Ingolfur Arnarson and his brother-in-law. Allegedly these two men had to give up their lands in Norway as recompense for the killing of a nobleman's son, and they longed for the wide-open spaces described by Flóki. In 870, they set sail for the new land. On arrival, the two men explored the country, and although his brother-in-law was eventually murdered by his own slaves, Ingolfur settled in 'Smoky Bay' – Reykja-vik – named for the distinctive plumes of smoke (wrongly identified pillars of steam, rising from the thermal waters).

Icelandic history is notable for the establishment of the world's first Parliament, the *Althingi*, at Thingvellir in 930. The early 13th century was a time of violent naval action, with sea battles being waged almost nonstop for nearly 50 years. Finally, Norway seized the island, and Iceland became simply a place for the Norwegians to raid. By the mid-14th century, the colonising country was devastated by a series of epidemics, including the Black Death, and Denmark took the opportunity to seize control of both Norway and Iceland. For the next four hundred years, Iceland went through some of its hardest times, with the Danes taking over Norway's role as plunderers. Disease and natural disasters ravaged whatever was left.

However, in the 18th century, the establishment of the *Innréttingar* provided the first hope for modernisation. With Danish support, the Royal Treasurer, Skúli Magnússon, set up 'Enterprises' – a company whose aims were to instigate an economic rebirth in Iceland. Foreign craftsmen arrived in Reykjavik, and although fishing, agriculture, shipbuilding and sulphur mining were among the projects undertaken, wool working proved the most successful of them and lasted well into the 1800s. Much of the city's physical development stemmed from this period, yet only one building remains untouched: Adalstræti 10 is virtually original. In 1786, Reykjavik was granted town status.

The Althingi was abolished in 1798, but in 1845 Denmark granted Iceland a certain degree of autonomy, and the Icelandic Parliament was restarted. The country's capital, Reykjavik, became the seat of government. Previously isolated, the legalislation of free trade to all nations proved a turning point in Iceland's commercial development

⊙ *Artefacts from the National Museum relate the city's history and traditions*

in 1855. Despite its long-standing official existence as a town, the first true council was set up in 1836, and by 1908, women were granted the right of vote in municipal elections.

World War I made no great impact on Iceland, but in the spring of 1940 British troops occupied the country. Reykjavik's population nearly doubled, with the addition of the United Kingdom military. The United States took over the job in 1941 and unemployment disappeared virtually overnight with work springing from the occupation. Following a referendum, Iceland declared independence from Denmark on 17 June 1944, with the previously acting Regent Sveinn Björnsson elected as president.

Reykjavik embraced the future, becoming a modern city. A great deal of this forward thinking was due to new technology involving the harnessing of Iceland's vast hydroelectric and geothermal energy. Power was, and still is, produced cleanly and renewably: electricity via the plentiful water resources; heat via the tapping of the country's thermal pools and springs. Much of the resulting revenue was channelled into the arts. The National Theatre began in 1950, as well as the Symphony Orchestra.

In the 1960s, Loftleidir, now Icelandair, began transatlantic flights with a free stopover in Keflavik, Reykjavik's airport. This perk brought the city to the attention of a globetrotting public, and helped overcome the Icelanders' sense of isolation from the outside world. The city breaks continue to this day.

Today, Reykjavik thrives, is affluent, clean and welcoming. The city has a sense of history, with its 9th-century settlement and 10th-century parliament. Yet having gained its independence in the 20th century, the country feels very young. Iceland has a very appealing combination of age in its tradition and of youth in its forward thinking.

THE WESTMANN ISLANDS

In November 1963, just off the south coast of Iceland and close to the major fishing port of the Westmann Islands, fishermen noticed the first rumblings of an offshore volcano. For three and a half years the eruption continued, and when the flow finally stopped, a land mass rising 169 m (555 ft) out of the sea had been created. The island was named Surtsey, after Surtur, a Norse fire-wielding god. Even before the lava cooled, Surtsey had been declared an area of special scientific interest, and offlimits to casual human visitors so that scientists could study implantation methods and bird migration patterns of the newest island on earth. Today, plants have taken root and several bird species nest here. Many more birds stop over on their way to other parts of the world.

Just under ten years later, on 23 January 1973, a huge fissure opened suddenly and unexpectedly, close to the main Westmann Islands' town of Heimaey. A mass evacuation commenced, with people hurriedly being flown and shipped over to the mainland. Two months later, the fire brigade installed a series of pipes and hoses so that the encroaching lava, which threatened to block the country's most productive southern port, could be diverted away from the mouth of the harbour. In July the eruption halted, with the island almost 30 per cent larger than it had been in January, and nearly half the town covered with volcanic material. The re-channelled lava made the harbour better than ever.

Lifestyle

Reykjavikingurs live well. The city is small yet has almost every major European store. The locals love to buy things, and fine art galleries pepper the main shopping street of the town. Goods are of very high quality, and readily purchased. Design is smart and evident

⬤ *Relaxing in hot pots and spas is all part of the local lifestyle*

everywhere – the Icelanders embrace their Norse traditions for style and carry it even further. Reykjavik is known for its coffee houses, restaurants, pubs and clubs, and the residents are not reluctant to patronise them. With the apparent lack of polluting industry, the frequent rain that cleanses the air, the beautiful mountain and sea vistas and the general feeling of healthiness, the city feels more like a resort than a capital.

The catch is the price. Iceland varies from being expensive to very expensive depending on the exchange rate. Costs are high, with alcohol and petrol particularly pricey. The government taxes these items particularly heavily, as disincentives. Alcohol abuse is a problem, especially during the long winter nights, while petrol must be imported. Nevertheless, people party enthusiastically throughout the year, buying their drinks from the national wine shop before and after attending the pub, to save a few Kronur. Most people own cars, with a large number of them 'gas guzzling' four-wheel drives, a real necessity in the countryside.

Salaries are high, but not in proportion to the additional costs. Taxation is also considerable, but health care is free, as is education. Icelanders, and especially the partying Rekjavikingurs, cope by taking on more than one job, often more than two. Just about every working person does two or three things for a living. Sometimes the occupations have nothing to do with each other, such as an industrial consultant who also runs owner-operated SuperJeep tours (who else could afford to buy the vehicle in the first place?) or an actor who also escorts camping groups. The locals themselves admit that life is expensive, but usually the second job is something a bit more fun than the first. It's hard to tell whether they accept this way of life because they have to, or whether they have found a way to afford and enjoy their lives.

Culture

For such a small city, Reykjavik has a very large number of cultural venues. The admission fees for several of the major museums and art galleries are included with the purchase of Reykjavik Tourist card (see page 63; also part of the package are bus fares and entrance to the public thermally heated swimming pools). The institutions covered are usually the national museums. The National Gallery holds the main collection of Icelandic art, as well as some 19th- and 20th-century examples. The Kjarvalstadir presents the work of one of the most popular landscape painters, Johannes Kjarval, while the Asmundursafn exhibits Asmundur Sveinnson's sculptures in his extraordinary house. More radical modern art is shown at the multi-functional Hafnarhús, and the Sigurjón Ólafsson Museum is in the artist's own studio. The Árbærsafn is the city's outdoor assembly of historic buildings, mostly from central Reykjavik, gathered in a semi-rural area of fields and farms, not far from the centre. The Culture House houses some original medieval manuscripts of the Icelandic sagas as well as some changing exhibitions, while Reykjavik Zoo and Family Park is just fun for the family.

The jewel in the city's cultural crown is the newly revamped National Museum of Iceland. State of the art, with beautifully presented displays (and an excellent coffee house), the museum describes the history of Iceland.

Smaller, private galleries abound, with artists exhibiting their own work. The main shopping street, Laugavegur, contains several of them. Nearby, Skóvöordustigur, punctuated by the dramatic Hallgrimskirkja church at the top of the street, is developing a

⏵ *The majestic interior of Hallgrimskirkja is just the venue for musical events*

reputation as something of an 'art' street, with painting, ceramic and fabric stores lining its pavements.

Reykjavik has a National Opera, Symphony Orchestra and Theatre each performing regularly all year round, although the number of events increases outside the summer tourist season. Iceland has a thriving music scene, with an extraordinary number of both professional and amateur jazz and rock groups featured in clubs and pubs.

Artistic events happen at any time of the year, the highlight being late August's Culture Night. The city opens up its galleries, museums, music and theatrical venues, and impromptu performers do their thing(s) from early morning till long past midnight (see page 34). Other happenings on the annual calendar include festivals that celebrate sacred arts, dance, tango, literature, film, jazz, rock and pop and most other forms of entertainment. Even Hallgrimskirkja church, Reykjavik's logo and unmistakeable icon, shows off its acoustics with the occasional concert.

ADMISSION CHARGES

The city's museums all incur a fee, although the purchase of a Reykjavik Tourist card includes several admissions. The Kjarvalstadir, Asmundursafn and Hafnarhus can all be visited in the same day for one entrance charge. Entry to the galleries' shops is usually free. Pubs and clubs usually do not charge a fee to listen to live music, but the purchase of at least one drink is expected.

● *The modern interior of The Pearl belies its origin as water tanks*

Shopping

The sense of Reykjavik being small, yet having virtually everything one could want, extends to its shopping. The city centre is full of delightful boutiques, craft shops, fine fashion venues, souvenir stalls and even convenience food markets. Slightly further afield are huge shopping malls with international brand-name as well as Icelandic specialist stores. There is even a huge weekend flea market for bargains and offbeat items.

Laugavegur is central Reykjavik's most prominent street and its prime shopping area. Narrow, so that cars have to drive slowly (if not give up and take alternative routes), it feels almost like a pedestrian precinct. Shops line its entire length, the slightly downmarket and funkier ones further away from the centre, the more exclusive ones highly visible closer to the city's heart. Much of the street's focus is on clothing. At the financially (but not physically) lower end of the street, it's possible to find secondhand goods and quirky items appealing to a younger crowd. As the street continues, the fashion becomes more exotic, with Icelandic design and one-off items being sold. Side lanes begin to branch off, with exclusive fashion and jewellery sandwiched between the fine art galleries. Dropping down in the direction of the harbour, brand names such as Prada begin to appear among the cafés (great for a break among all this commerce). 66° North, Iceland's high-quality, weather gear producers, has one of its more prominent show stores here.

Once near the main square, the one-off shops disappear and are replaced by souvenir venues, offering mostly Icelandic woollen goods. It's possible to pick up cheaper – and less practical – goods,

● *Kringlan mall offers every retail experience the visitor could want*

such as toy puffins, 'Iceland' T-shirts and photography books, sometimes on sale.

Bookshops are scattered along the length of the shopping streets, and they also sell foreign newspapers. Books are sold in several languages, but English titles dominate the non-Icelandic publications.

Further away are the huge shopping malls. Kringlan, located near the geographical, if not tourist, centre of greater Reykjavik, is an archetypal centre with 170 shops and restaurants. Also here are

A viking helmet may be just the souvenir for you to take home

pharmacies, banks, doctors' offices, a food court and a multi-screen movie theatre. Smaralind is in Kópavogur, the capital city's next-door neighbour and still within public transport distance. With boasts of being the largest shopping centre in Iceland and on the way to Keflavik (Reykjavik's international airport), the mall has the usual shops and businesses as well as a huge hypermarket, Hagkaup.

At weekends, Reykjavik's flea market down by the harbour, Kolaportid, comes to life. A huge warehouse full of secondhand clothing, rock memorabilia, book stores and kitsch items, the market is a popular place to stroll among Reykjavik's castoffs. In the back is a section for strange Icelandic food specialities, including salt cod, *hardfiskur* (dried fish which the locals eat like crisps) and even *Hakarl*, the rotted shark speciality bearable only with a shot of *brennevin*, the Icelandic high-octane spirit.

USEFUL SHOPPING PHRASES

What time do the shops open/close?
Hvenær er opnad/lokad?
Kvehnehr ehrr opnahth/lokahth?

How much is it?
Hvad kostar?
Kvahth kostahrr?

I'd like to buy ...
Mig langar ad kaupa ...
Mikh lownkhahr ahth ke-erpah ...

Eating & drinking

What Reykjavik lacks in inexpensive options for eating, it virtually overcompensates for in gastronomic variety. The choice of restaurants, cafés, bistros, bars, pubs and even fast food outlets is huge, especially for what seems to be such a small city. Most tastes and nationalities are catered for, with American, Asian, Danish, French, Italian and vegetarian venues especially well covered. Of course, Icelandic cuisine is highly regarded, with the excellent resources of fish, seafood and lamb being featured. It's possible to save money by visiting the local supermarkets for picnic lunch foods and between-meal snacks, although prices here are also fairly high. Try to avoid the convenience stores and aim for the proper food stores.

Many restaurants are open all day from about 11.00 to late in the evening. Some places open for dinner at around 18.00. Occasionally a particular place can open a little early for the evening meal, offering an early-bird special to encourage diners (and poor tourists) to patronise an establishment before the usual evening crowds appear. Closing times are dependent on how busy the restaurant is, and final

---

PRICE RATING

The restaurant price guides used in the book indicate the approximate cost of a three-course meal for one person, excluding drinks, at the time of writing.

£ up to 2220Kr.   ££ 2220–4500Kr.   £££ more than 4500Kr.

● *Seafood – of all shapes and sizes – is a staple of the local cuisine*

orders can sometimes be very late indeed.

Generally, prices are high, and there are practically no exceptions. Eating out is expensive but quality is good almost everywhere. Fine cuisine is the standard, and once the shock of seeing the cost on the menu, let alone later on the final bill, is overcome, the experience is a pleasure. Tipping is not part of local custom, and rarely done. Locals dress well and this fashion consciousness is reflected in their evening attire, although dress codes are not usually enforced in restaurants. If diners appear at the door in jeans and hiking boots, they will not be turned away, but will definitely be identified as tourists.

Cafés are an essential part of Reykjavik life to both the locals and tourists. It's possible to order a cafetiere or designer latte and spend long hours in one place, sipping that long-deserved cup of coffee, conducting business or merely people-watching. Many of the city's cafés are chameleons, serving java, then food, then becoming clubs in the evening. This transition can happen nonstop, with service and customers slipping almost seamlessly into the next phase. Coffee houses that really do specialise in coffee only tend to start early and close around 18.00. Cafés usually open around 11.00 and close when they want, around 01.00 on weekdays and up to 06.00 – or later – at weekends.

DRINKING

Alcohol is particularly expensive, with a bottle of house wine at a restaurant regularly costing around £20.00/2200Kr. and up. Nevertheless, ordering drinks to accompany a meal is fairly common, although excessive consumption is rare. Clubs and pubs serve beverages at the same prices, and do good business.

◐ *Your chef may not wear the usual hat if there is something to celebrate*

Locals often start early, purchasing their bottles at the state-run off licences, *Vinbudin*, and beginning their drinking at home.

FAST FOOD & DO-IT-YOURSELF

Reykjavik has a high number of takeaway and fast-food eateries. Names such as Domino's, Kentucky Fried Chicken, McDonald's and Pizza Hut are familiar, while the Icelandic equivalents are just as prevalent. Be careful, though, as a McDonald's meal can still be quite pricey. Pizza, for some unexplained reason, is particularly expensive, with a meal and a coke creeping into the **££** category. The city's best food bargain is a hot dog (*pylsur*) and it's possible to find a decent one for less than £1.00/110Kr.

Purchasing food at supermarkets is a reasonable option, particularly away from the city centre. Convenience stores such as 1011 are just that, with long hours and good locations, but their prices are comparatively high. Larger supermarkets, such as Bonus and Hagkaup, are better value but harder to find. Street markets offer quality and organic produce and as such cost a bit more.

LOCAL SPECIALITIES

Iceland is justly proud of some of its local food, particularly fish and lamb. The former is often found as salt cod, the dried then reconstituted chunk of fish that is found in many regional dishes. Lamb, too, is delicious, and can be eaten economically in the traditional hearty meat and veg soup common at lunch (and especially good on those cold, wet days).

Seabirds are fairly common on the menu, with puffin being the most prevalent. Often served smoked, the taste has been compared to veal. More fun, however, are the weird, uniquely Icelandic dishes sold mostly at speciality restaurants. *Hákarl* is rotten shark meat, served in tiny chunks, and virtually inedible. It smells horrible, but tastes worse, and is usually consumed with generous portions of *brennivin*, a powerful and taste-numbing spirit. Pickled ram's testicles, served commonly as a sort of pâté, and cod chins or cheeks, taken from the fish's head, are legacies from the days when almost anything was considered edible.

USEFUL DINING PHRASES

I would like a table for ... people, please.
Get ég fengid ... manna bord?
Gyeht yehkh fayngith ...mahnah borrth?

May I see the menu, please?
Get ég fengid ad sjá matsedilinn?
Gyeht yehkh fayngith ahth syow mahtsethilin?

I am a vegetarian.
Ég er grænmetisæta.
Yehkh ehrr grain-mehtisaitah.

Where is the toilet (restroom) please?
Hvar er snyrtingin?
Kvahr ehrr snirrinkhin?

May I have the bill, please?
Ég vil borga reikninginn.
Yehkh vil borkhah rraykninkhin.

Entertainment & nightlife

BARS, CLUBS & PUBS

Reykjavik is legendary for its bar, club and pub nightlife and justifiably so. As with most of the city's commodities, the number of such venues is disproportionately high for such a small population. The inhabitants like to party. Most of the action happens at weekends, when the bars close at 03.00, 04.00, 05.00 or even later, depending on how the party is going (on weekdays, places close around 01.00). Nothing much really happens until midnight, when some clubs and bars begin to

charge an entry fee. To avoid the payment, arrive early, brave the lack of action, and hang out until things happen. The clubs will not ask for money, nor throw out sitting clientele.

The secret to the festivities is to choose the right place. The bars that are in vogue change on a regular basis and what is 'in' one month will not necessarily be 'the' place the next. Check the monthly guides to see the trends, or ask the locals. Places are generally geared to particular criteria; for example, age, dress, locals,

As night falls, many cafés metamorphose into clubs and bars

tourists, food, music, drinking, chat, meeting others or simply
hanging out with friends. It's a sophisticated system.

Generally, locals go home after work and relax a bit, giving them
the opportunity to dress up before going out. They often begin their
alcohol consumption at home where it's cheaper, or at informal
gatherings at friends' houses. By the time they reach the bar, the
initial drinking is done, so that the high cost of alcohol isn't so
damaging. Nevertheless, the locals party hard, and prices don't
diminish consumption. Favourite places are often chosen by who
the Reykjavikingurs think will be where. The city is small, and most
people know each other, as is evident by the handshakes and
rousing hellos that greet arrivals. Foreigners can be welcomed, or
ignored, depending on various things, such as how tight the regular
group is, how well the visitors are dressed, how open both the locals
and visitors are, or any number of reasons. In general, people are
friendly, although they can be a little aloof.

OTHER ENTERTAINMENT

Despite the reputation for clubbing, Reykjavik has alternatives for
night-time entertainment. **The City Theatre** (ⓐ Borgarleikhus
Listabraut 3 ☎ 568 8000 ⓦ www.borgarleikhus.is) and **National
Theatre** (ⓐ Hverfisgötu ☎ 551 1200 ⓦ www.leikhusid.is) are
professional companies that put on regular productions. There are
several other theatre groups offering performances, some in
English.

As well as rock bands and jazz groups, the **National Opera**
(ⓐ Ingólfsstræti ☎ 511 4200 ⓦ www.opera.is) and the **Iceland
Symphony Orchestra** (ⓐ Háskólabíó (University Cinema) ☎ 545 2500
ⓦ www.sinfonia.is) offer more formal musical opportunities.

Cinema is extremely popular, with many of the films being

shown in their original language. US and UK movies are not usually dubbed. For more information, check out ⓦ www.visitreykjavik.is.

ENTERTAINMENT LISTINGS

There is no shortage of information on Reykjavik. Most accessible is the website for the Reykjavik Tourist Board (ⓦ www.visitreykjavik.is) which includes up-to-date listings. Tourist booklets, such as *Reykjavik City Guide* (ⓦ www.icelandtoday.is) and *What's On in Reykjavik* (ⓦ www.whatson.is), are updated monthly.

The street mag, *The Reykjavik Grapevine* (ⓦ www.grapevine.is) is very useful. General Icelandic publications updated seasonally, such as the *Visitor's Guide* (ⓦ www.visitorsguide.is) and the Iceland Information Human guides are also extremely helpful.

YOUR FRIEND FOR THE NIGHT

If the prospect of trying to break into the club scene is a bit intimidating, especially for a short break, 'Your Reykjavik Nightlife Friend' could be a help. A legitimate tour guide, Jon Kari Hilmarsson offers a quick entry into Reykjavik's night-time party life. Knowing both the travel industry from his work experience, as well as, what seems to be, most of the people in Reykjavik, he has taken his passion for the bar life and blended it into a different way of seeing the city.

Recommended by the tourist board, Jon Kari meets his clients ahead of time to see what they would like and then shows them around to places he feels are appropriate. Contact 'Your Rekjavik Nightlife Friend' on ☎ 692 1003 ⓦ www.nightlifefriend.is.

Sport & relaxation

SPECTATOR SPORTS

The two main sports that Reykjavingurs like to watch are football (soccer) and handball. Iceland has produced a surprisingly good football team, with a following as enthusiastic as any other in Europe. Handball, too, gets a good crowd and Reykjavik was host to the world championship in 1995.

Both these disciplines hold their games at the main sports stadium in Laugardalur Valley. For more information regarding dates and times, contact the tourist board. Interestingly enough, close to the stadium, in the Laugardalsholl sports hall, the famous chess match between the Soviet Boris Spassky and the American Bobby Fisher was held in 1972.

PARTICIPATION & RELAXATION

Laugardalur Valley is the centre of many of Reykjavik's sporting activities, not only for professional teams but also for amateur enthusiasts. As well as including running tracks, football fields and an indoor ice rink, there are also the largest thermal pool and gym in the city, as well as a brand-new and extremely upmarket spa.

Angling is very popular, although it can be extremely expensive. Salmon fishing is one of Iceland's largest tourist revenue earners. Despite the fact that the best rivers are outside the city and have to be booked years in advance, fish have been caught in the Ellidaár, the river that runs through Reykjavik. Trout fishing permits are available for a small fee, and can be used in lakes throughout Iceland.

Reykjavik's closest golf course is on a lava-strewn green of the Keilir Golf club in the nearby city of Hafnarfjördur (W www.keilir.is).

The best-known venue, however, is in the northern city of Akureyri, where the all-night Arctic Open is held on the summer solstice, in virtual 24-hour daylight (ⓦ www.arcticopen.is).

Iceland is a hikers' paradise, with many of the best areas reached on a day trip from the city. Locally, the best bet for a good stiff climb is to walk up Mt Esja, the mountain that faces Reykjavík from across the bay. It takes from 1–3 hours to reach the summit at 900 m (2700 ft) above sea level. From the centre of Reykjavik, take bus no. 15 to Mossfellsbaer (a town just to the northeast), then transfer to bus no. 27 to reach the foot of the mountain.

Horse-riding excursions are very popular, particularly on the

SPA CITY

One of the resources upon which Iceland sits, the natural hot springs generated by volcanic activity, has been harnessed to create a favourite national activity – sitting in geothermal waters. Although some in the country are natural occurring, in Reykjavik what appear to be swimming pools are actually comfortably heated thermal pools. Alongside are 'hot pots', or whirlpool-like baths. Traditionally, locals can spend hours here, often discussing politics. The pools are popular winter and summer, and are surprisingly inexpensive (and included in the Reykjavik Card).

A very precise etiquette accompanies the use of spa pools. Entrants are required to shower thoroughly with soap beforehand without a swimsuit in order to ensure the hygiene of the pool itself, then put the suit back on before entering the water. There are seven of these public pools in Reykjavik.

● *The Icelandic horse has a placid nature – great for novice riders*

unique Icelandic horses. An ancient breed, they have two special gaits, including a running walk – the *tölt* – that is particularly suited to riding long trails. Based in the city, tours are offered in the nearby countryside. Thyrill is one company (Thyrill – Vididalur Hraunbær ⓐ 2, Reykjavik 110 , ❶ 567 3370, Ⓦ www.thyrill.is) but there are several others. Check with the tourist office for details.

Skidoo excursions are available all year round. Tours by coach, or even better by Superjeep, take visitors to the glaciers, where skidoos are waiting. Day trips are available from Activity Group (Ⓦ www.activity.is), Discover the World (Ⓦ www.dtw.is), Iceland Excursions (Ⓦ www.icelandexcursions.is) and Mountain Taxi, (Ⓦ www.mountaintaxi.is), among others.

Skiing is a popular sport in Iceland, and from November to April, if there is good snow, three ski resorts operate around Reykjavik: Blafjoll, Hengill and Skálafell (www.skidasvaedi.is). However, most people head north for Akureyri's winter sports area (www.hlidarfjall.is), where snow is more likely and the facilities are better.

Whale-watching has arrived in Reykjavik, and seagoing excursions are available to see dolphins, humpback, minke and orca whales, and seals. What is actually viewed – no guarantees are made – depends on the season. Destination Iceland (www.dice.is), Elding Whale Watching (www.elding.is) and Whale Watching Centre (www.whalewatching.is) all leave from the Old Harbour. Further north, in Husavik, the 'Whale Watching Capital of Europe', there is a 98 per cent record of sea mammal viewing when the boats go out. Here, North Sailing (www.nordursigling.is) and Gentle Giants (www.gentlegiants.is) are the companies that sail.

○ *A whale-watching trip may be a rewarding experience...*

Accommodation

Reykjavik is pricey and the costs for accommodation are no exception. As a compensation, the standard of facilities, cleanliness and hospitality is high, whether in a youth hostel or in the fanciest hotel in town. Neighbouring communities have less expensive guesthouses, although the number of these outlying places to stay is quite limited and the locations comparatively far from the centre. Within central Reykjavik, accommodation is plentiful.

Watch out for festivals and special events when spaces are filled very quickly (by out-of-town Icelanders, as well as foreign tourists). It's wise to book well ahead in such cases. The tourist board online, at Ⓦ www.visitreykjavik.is, has a comprehensive listing with excellent links to the individual lodgings.

Despite the tourist board's successful attempts to introduce Reykjavik as a low-season winter, as well as a high-season summer, destination, rates drop as much as 25 per cent from October to April. Prices are generally two-tier, with hotel stays in the colder months proving to be much more affordable. Unless travelling with a group or on a package tour, discounts are not generally offered for longer durations. Breakfast is almost always included.

Guesthouses offer a more intimate and personable alternative to the bigger and smarter hotels, although the price difference isn't always a great deal. Like Bed & Breakfasts, which are cheaper, it's a good way to get to know a few more Rekjavikingurs. Many guesthouses have shared bathroom facilities. Some even offer dorm rooms and kitchen areas to reduce living costs still further.

Both Reykjavik and the nearby town of Hafnarfjördur have a campsite and a HI youth hostel. In the capital, these facilities are in the Laugardalur Valley, a bus ride away from the centre. Prices here

PRICE RATING

All are approximate prices for a single night in a double room/two persons during the summer season (May-September).

£ up to 8900Kr.; **££** 8900–14,500Kr.; **£££** 14,500Kr. and over

are not as low as one would expect, and visitors often prefer the convenience, and not much higher cost, of staying in a dorm room in a guesthouse in town.

The Star system is used by only a few hotels, and therefore not comprehensively representative.

GUESTHOUSES

101 Guesthouse £ With spacious rooms and shared facilities, this modern guesthouse is located within minutes of the main shopping street. ⓐ Laugavegur 101 101 ⓣ 562 6101 ⓕ 562 6105 ⓦ www.travelnet.is

Adam Guesthouse £ The newly renovated rooms are equipped with bathrooms, basic kitchens and free internet, and are situated on the 'art street'. ⓐ Skólavördustígur 42 101 ⓣ 896 0242 ⓕ 551 1506 ⓦ www.adam.is

Centrum Guesthouse £ Close to the centre as well as to the Art Museum and bus terminal, a nice thermal pool is just around the corner. ⓐ Njálsgata 74 101 ⓣ 511 5600 ⓕ 511 5611 ⓦ www.guesthouse-centrum.com

Domus Guesthouse £ In an old building in the heart of the centre, Domus has 12 double rooms and a shared kitchen, as well as space for 22 in sleeping bags. ⓐ Hverfisgata 45 101 ① 561 1200 ❶ 561 1201 Ⓦ www.domusguesthouse.is

Floki Guesthouse £ Slightly off the beaten track, this friendly guesthouse is still close to most of what the city has to offer. ⓐ Flókagata 1 105 ① 552 1155 ❶ 562 0355 Ⓦ www.eyjar.is/guesthouse

Guesthouse Helguhus £ In the neighbouring town of Hafnarfjördur, Helguhus is located in a quiet and peaceful area. ⓐ Lækjarkinn 8 220 ① 555 2842 Ⓦ www.helguhus.is

Guesthouse Isafold £ Well placed in old – and quieter – Reykjavik, Isafold is still close to the best of the city's activities. ⓐ Bárugata 11 101 ① 561 2294 ❶ 562 9965 Ⓦ www.itn.is/~isafold

Kriunes Guesthouse £ Further away and close to Lake Ellidavatn, this virtual mansion blends the quiet of the countryside with relative proximity to the capital. ⓐ Vid Vatnsenda 203 ① 567 2245 ❶ 567 2226 Ⓦ www.kriunes.is

Salvation Army Guesthouse £ Incredibly situated, right in the heart of town, here it's possible to bed down in a single, double or triple room, as well as in sleeping-bag accommodation. ⓐ Kirkjustræti 2 101 ① 561 3203 ❶ 561 3315 Ⓦ www.guesthouse.is

Snorri's Guesthouse £ Close to both the Flybus city terminus and Laugavegur, Reykjavik's main shopping street, Snorri's is within

● *If you want a cheaper option, consider sleeping-bag accomodation*

walking distance of an number of attractions. ● Snorrabraut 61 105
● 552 0598 ● 551 8945 ● www.guesthousereykjavik.com

HOTELS

Hotel Fron £ This new apartment hotel is situated on Laugavegur,
the city's main shopping street. ● Klapparstígur 35a 101 ● 511 4666
● 511 4665 ● www.hotelfron.is

Fosshotel Baron ££ With stunning views across the bay, the Baron is a comfortable tourist-class hotel close to Reykjavik's harbour.
ⓐ Baronstígur 2-4 101, ① 552 4488 ① 562 4001
ⓦ www.fosshotel.is/fosshotel-english.htm

Hotel Björk ££ This affordable – by Reykjavik standards – hotel has all basic facilities and is part of the quality Kea chain.
ⓐ Brautarholt 22-24 105 ① 511 3777 ① 511 3776 ⓦ www.keahotels.is

Hotel Leifur Eiríksson ££ Under the shadow of Hallgrimskirkja church, the city's dominant building, the small and friendly Leifur Eiríksson has nicely furnished rooms. ⓐ Skólavördustígur 45 101
① 562 0800 ① 562 0800 ⓦ www.hotelleifur.is/english/

Hotel Reykjavík ££ Comfortable, modern and close to the main bus station, this hotel is within walking distance of most of what there is to see in the city. ⓐ Raudarárstígur 37 105 ① 514 7000 ① 514 7030
ⓦ www.hotelreykjavik.is

101 Hotel £££ The emphasis is on design and in-house facilities in this new boutique hotel right in the centre of the city. ⓐ Hverfisgata 10 101 ① 580 0101 ① 580 0100 ⓦ www.101hotel.is

Hotel Borg £££ Dominating Austurvöllur Square, the 75-year-old Hotel Borg has long been a central Reykjavik landmark. Since its opening, this hotel has been the place to stay, whether for visiting dignitaries or for the more affluent tourist who wanted to have a true urban Icelandic experience.

At the height of fashion, for its time, the art deco style and details have been preserved, the recently renovated facilities are certainly up to 21st-century standards, and it yet upholds its reputation for modern luxury. @ Pósthússtræti 11 101 @ 551 1440 @ 551 1420 @ www.hotelborg.is

Hotel Loftleidir Icelandair £££ Icelandair's quality venue is a good place to stay for a bit of indulgence, with indoor swimming pool, solarium and massage suite, although it is a little way from the city centre. @ Hlidarfótur 101 @ 444 4500 @ 444 4501 @ www.icehotels.is

● *The original art deco style of Hotel Borg is still evident*

THE BEST OF REYKJAVIK

Whether you are on a flying visit to Reykjavik or have a little more time to explore the city and its surroundings, there are some sights, places and experiences that you should not miss. For the best attractions for children, see pages 149–151.

TOP 10 ATTRACTIONS

- **Laugavegur** The city's main shopping street is lined with picturesque shops and houses (see page 74).

- **Hallgrimskirkja** A church disguised as a space ship is the city's most recognisable landmark (see page 72).

- **National Museum of Iceland (Thjódminjasafn)** Recently renovated into a fine state-of-the-art museum, its exhibits describe anything anyone could ever want to know about the history of the country (see page 76).

- **Culture House** Superb original medieval manuscripts of the Icelandic sagas are displayed within this city centre museum (see page 75).

- **Whale-watching and puffin tours** Magnificent giant mammals and comic, colourful birds can be spotted while cruising Reykjavik's beautiful bay (see page 41).

- **Café society** Whether sitting outside on a warm day, or inside on a cold, coffee drinking and people watching is a national must.

- **Thermal pools** Natural geothermal energy heats these public swimming pools and provides an inexpensive and delightful spa experience (see page 39).

- **Pub and club culture** Find out what makes Reykjavik's nightlife so legendary (see page 34).

- **Festivals** Art, culture, food and historical festivals happen any time of the year (see pages 9–11).

- **Nature at the door** Much of Iceland's spectacular scenery is available a mere day trip away (see page 106).

◆ *Iceland's majestic mountain scenery looms over its capital city*

Your brief guide to seeing the best that Reykjavik has to offer, depending on how much time you have.

HALF-DAY: REYKJAVIK IN A HURRY

Stroll down Laugavegur, perusing the more offbeat shops at the more downmarket end and admiring the fine art and design as the route approaches the city's centre. Perhaps stop at one of the main coffee houses, Kaffitár or Café Solon for example, on the way. Continue to the old harbour and view the fishing boats. Turn back and walk through the Old Town, or through Austurvöllur Square, the city's traditional heart. Walk towards the modern City Hall (Radhús), maybe stepping inside to see the free exhibition. Continue along the banks of the City Pond (Tjörnin) to enjoy the fine views and feed the ducks.

1 DAY: TIME TO SEE A LITTLE MORE

With a bit more time, visit one or more of the museums, some worth a whole day to themselves. The National Museum is excellent for Iceland's history, while the Culture House shows off original medieval manuscripts.

Reykjavik also has several fine art galleries, which are certainly worth viewing. The Kjarvalstadir is the best known of the triumvirate of art museums (together with the more radical Hafnarhús and the Asmundursafn sculpture garden), which can be entered on a single day ticket.

Whale watching is a good option for spending an afternoon during the season, preferably on a calm day. An excellent way to finish off the afternoon is by visiting one of Reykjavik's seven thermal pools, all open to the public.

2–3 DAYS: SHORT CITY-BREAK

For longer stays, investing in a Reykjavik Tourist Card (available for 24- or 72-hour durations) is a good idea, as this card provides entry to most of the city's museums and swimming pools, as well as free transport on the buses plus internet access at the city centre. A morning to spare might be worth allowing for recovery from the previous night's indulgence in Reykjavik's pub and club life.

One day should certainly be spent in an excursion to some of the country's incredible scenic spots. The Golden Circle includes the historic and geological site of Thingvellir, the erupting hot springs of Geysir and the beautiful Gullfoss waterfall, and can be visited by organised tour or rental car.

Alternatively, an easier day can be spent at the Blue Lagoon resort, a gigantic hot spring pool fed by the runoff of a geothermal power station.

LONGER: ENJOYING REYKJAVIK TO THE FULL

There are so many festivals happening in Reykjavik that an extended stay is bound to overlap some event. More time would allow the opportunity of seeing the opera, symphony or National Theatre in action. In addition, the city is an excellent base for exploring the rest of Iceland, with several tour companies offering both single and multi-day tours.

Snæfelsjökull, the glacier-capped mountain often visible in the distance across Reykjavik Bay's is excellent as a destination for both one and multi-day trips. A short flight, or longer drive, to Akureyri provides an excellent two-day (or more) option, as there are many extraordinary scenic spots within easy reach of Iceland's second city.

Something for nothing

Despite Reykjavik's often justified reputation for being expensive, the city is not unfriendly to those visitors who have little cash to spare. There are quite a few things to see and do that require no funds at all. Although the city limits encompass a large area, central Reykjavik is quite small, and most things to see are within walking distance. Probably the most fun thing to do is stroll, looking at the city's outdoor architecture and shop windows. If hunger strikes, though not quite free, hot dogs (*pylsur*) from places such as the fast-food outlet of Aktu Taktu are inexpensive and provide enough strength to continue the free tour. In the very centre is the City Hall, a modern building partially sitting astride the city pond. There are often exhibitions here and a fascinating giant relief map of the

● *Relaxation and recreation at Nautholsvik*

country. At weekends, the indoor Coal Port Market (Kolaportid), down by the harbour, is a huge flea market selling lots of weird and wonderful things, including old rock memorabilia, obscure Icelandic books and some of the country's more questionable gastronomic specialities

Hallsgrimkirkja is free and is open most of the day (although the climb to the top of the 75 m (250 ft) viewpoint incurs a small fee). The massive city church is an intriguing place to visit and it is sometimes possible to sit in on concert rehearsals.

Two museums, the National Gallery and the Asmundursafn (further afar in Laugardalur Valley) have free outdoor sculpture gardens to complement their interior collections. The Nordic House, which explains the Nordic cultures to locals as well as visitors, offers free entry to its exhibition hall. Reykjavik Museum of Photography also invites people in without charge. The Pearl (Perlan) in Öskjuhiid Hill is closer than it looks from town, and is a fairly easy walk. Entry to this complex, partially constructed from six hot water storage tanks, is free to the public, and a walk up to the top floor will provide one of the best views over the city. Just outside the city is Strokkur, an artificial copy of one of the more impressive geysers of the country. Further down the hill and past the domestic airport is a recreation area that includes Nautholsvik, the outdoor sand beach that has been roped off so that the water within is geothermally heated. On warm days the place is buzzing.

Somewhat of a walk is Kringlan, Reykjavik's giant shopping mall. Full of mainstream shops, food halls and lots of people, it's still a fun place to hang out if money is short. If the timing is right, many of the festivals are giant street parties, and with luck, music, performances and, sometimes, even food and drink samples are all offered with good grace and without charge.

When it rains

Being the northernmost capital city in Europe, and surrounded by the rain-bringing Gulf Stream, poor weather in Reykjavik is a common occurrence, and hardly changes the tourist itinerary. Much of what there is to see is equally fun to view with precipitation as with sun. With so much of interest in the city, rain often gives visitors a chance to peruse the art galleries and museums they would normally pass by. The Reykjavik Tourist Card includes entry to 14 cultural institutions. Shopping, too, becomes a pleasure when there is enough time to peruse the woollen clothing and photography books available only in Iceland. Then there are the things that the locals do themselves when the weather is unfriendly. On rainy days, Reykjavikingurs crowd into coffee houses, linger longer, and are often more chatty – even to visitors. There doesn't seem to be any rush and time slips away delightfully.

Spas and hot tubs are well patronised, and the outdoor thermal pools have even more attendees during rain than in sun. After all, one can't get any wetter! It might even be possible to get into a serious discussion with an Icelander, sitting in a very pleasantly warm outdoor 'hot pot' while the rain pours. If excess energy is an issue, the excellent gym of Laugardar is not only state of the art, but also a great place to be seen, and the hedonistic saunas, steam baths and showers of the adjoining Laugar Spa make all that hard work worth it.

The major museums are essentials, rain or shine, but some of the less-frequented galleries are worth a look, especially when it's wet outside. The centrally located Reykjavik Museum of Photography holds changing exhibitions and often shows images with Icelandic themes (see page 77). Further away but also very intriguing is the

Ásmundersafn (see page 96), the sculpture collection of Asmundur Sveinsson, a favourite son of the country. Although there are outdoor pieces, the indoor ones are not only more indicative of the maker's style, but show off the extraordinary artist-designed residence.

As rain falls, heading into the shops of central Reykjavik is one way to pass the time. Up and down Laugarvegur are unusual stores, while Skólavördustigur is known for its craft items. Kringlan mall, further away but completely undercover, is large enough to occupy a tourist in poor weather for a whole day at least (see page 101).

● *Take an intentional soaking at a spa in or out of the rain*

On arrival

TIME DIFFERENCES

Reykjavik is on Greenwich Mean Time (GMT) all year round. When it is 12.00 noon in the Icelandic summer, time at home is as follows:

Australia Eastern Standard Time 22.00, Central Standard Time 21.30, Western Standard Time 20.00

South Africa 14.00

New Zealand 22.00

UK 13.00

USA and Canada Newfoundland Time 09.30, Atlantic Canada Time 09.00, Eastern Time 07.00, Central Time 06.00, Mountain Time 05.00, Pacific Time 04.00, Alaska 03.00.

ARRIVING

By air

Visitors flying into Iceland arrive at Leifur Eiríksson Air Terminal, better known as Keflavik International airport. Reykjavik does have its own airport close to the city centre, but it handles domestic services only.

Leifur Eiríksson Air Terminal, Keflavik Airport (Ⓦ www.airport.is/english or Ⓦ www.keflavikairport.com), is in Keflavik, a small town approximately 50 km (31 miles) west of Reykjavik's city centre. The airport is extremely modern, offering a wide range of services to passengers. A post office, currency exchange, restaurants and duty-free sales (for both arriving and departing passengers) are available at the terminal.

The Flybus is the best way for most passengers to make their way into the city, although pre-booked holiday arrivals usually have transfers included in their packages. The service is tied in with arrivals and departures and takes 45–50 mins between the airport and its main BSI Coach Terminal in town. Most hotels and many guesthouses are on the itinerary and bus drivers will stop if informed in advance. Fares are approximately 1150Kronur one way for adults (and half-price for children). More information can be obtained from the flybus website  www.flybus.is or from  www.nat.is. Taxis are available, although far more expensive. The average fare to the centre of town in a four-seater taxi is around 7230Kr.

Most of the local car hire firms are represented at the airport at the arrivals area. Visitors who plan to explore the country first and return to Reykjavik later will find it convenient to obtain the vehicle

● Keflavik International Airport is some way out of town

from here rather than to make their arrangements in the city.

Reykjavik has a small domestic airport servicing Air Iceland. Located almost in the centre of the city, it's no more than a 5-min taxi ride from almost any hotel or guesthouse. Flights to different parts of the country leave from here.

Keflavik Airport Ⓦ www.airport.is
Air Iceland Ⓦ www.airiceland.is
Flybus Ⓦ www.flybus.is

By boat

Although most visitors choose to arrive by air, there is a regular scheduled passenger and car ferry service to the port at Seydisfördur in eastern Iceland. Smyril Lines are the operators. This somewhat convoluted journey takes three days from the UK, and goes via the Shetland and Faeroe Islands.

Smyril Lines Ⓦ www.smyril-line.com

From the port there are bus services to almost everywhere in Iceland, and the trip to Reykjavik, crossing the country from east to west, will take most of the day. For information on bus services outside the capital, visit Ⓦ www.nat.is/travelguideeng.

If travelling with a vehicle, to get to the capital the quickest way possible, take route 93 west to Egisstadir, then turn on to Iceland's ring road, route 1. It really doesn't matter much whether one heads north or south – both directions take a long time (and each leads through incredible scenery) and eventually arrive in Reykjavik.

Cruise ships that ply the arctic and have Iceland as one of their ports of call will arrive in Reykjavik. Ships dock at the Old Harbour, minutes away from the city centre. From there, everything worth seeing within the limited shore leave can be visited.

FINDING YOUR FEET

Central Reykjavik is very small and can be traversed on foot in half a day. Most things of tourist interest are within this area. However, the city officially covers 275 square km (900 sq ft), of which only 45 sq km (150 sq ft) are densely populated, and this can be a lot bigger than it first seems. What looks on the map to be very close might take longer to reach than expected.

Visits to tourist areas outside the centre, such as the Laugardalur or Ellidaár Valleys, are best made by public transport or car. Parts of the inner city are pedestrianised and car traffic here is slow.

Security wise, Reykjavik is probably one of the safest cities in Europe. Crime is rare and late-night walking in the tourist areas fine. Good sense is always advisable, but no special surveillance is necessary.

IF YOU GET LOST, TRY ...

Excuse me, do you speak English?
Afsakid, talar thú ensku?
Ahfsahkith, tahlahrr thoo ehnsker?

How do I get to ...?
Hvernig kemst ég til ...?
Kvehrrdnikh kyehmst yehkh til ...?

Can you show me on my map?
Getur thú s˘nt mér á kortinu?
Gehterr thoo sent myehrr ow korrtiner?

Nice Cafe Sægreifin
Lobstersoup!

Church

Old Harbour

Geirsgata

Kalkofnsv

Sæbraut

Túngata

Hverfisgata

Austurvöllur Square

Horsvallagata

Tjörnin

Fríkirkjuv

Soleyjargata

Suðurgata

Hallgrimskirkja

Snorrab

Kjarvalsst

Hringbraut

Miklab

Bústaðavegur

Einarsnes

✈ **Reykjavík Domestic Airport**

The Pearl & Saga Muse

ÖSKJUHLID

N

0   500m

Reykjavík.

Nauthólsvík

Sæbraut

Borartún

Sundlaugavegur

Laugar Spa

Laugardur Valley

Reykjavik Botanical Gardens

Nóatún

Laugavegur

Nóatún

Asmundursafn

Suðurlandsbraut

Family Park, Zoo and Science World

gata

Kringlumýrarbraut

Háaleitisbraut

Sambio Cinema

Kringlan

City Theatre

Miklabraut

Ellidaár Valley

Kringlumýrarbraut

Bústaðavegur

Arbaersafn & Energy Museum

↓ **Keflavik International Airport**

ORIENTATION

Reykjavik is on a peninsula jutting westward into the ocean. The suburban areas of Ellidaár and Laugardalur are to the east, and the city centre is to the west, nestling against the bayside harbour to the north. Just to the west of the centre and resting along the seaside is a residential area, and directly south of the city's heart is the domestic airport. On its east side is the recreational area of Öskjuhlid, site of the Pearl and Nautholsvik Beach.

Laugavegur is the street of most interest to the visitor and it runs east-northwest, beginning almost as far east as Laugadalur Valley. Running west parallel to the shoreline (some streets to the north), it doesn't start to offer any tourist attractions till just past Hlemmur, the site of one of Reykjavik's two main bus stations. To the south and up the hill the dramatic Hallgrimskirkja Church, Reykjavik's most visible landmark, comes into view. Continuing on Lagavegur, the street then gets quite narrow, and heads downhill till it crosses Læjargata. Here, the name changes briefly to Bankstræti. To the west is where the pedestrian area begins.

Just to the south of Austurstræti (Laugavegur/Bankastræti's new name) is Austurvöllur Square. Straight ahead is the open area of Adalstræti where much of Reykjavik's festival life takes place, and on the opposite side of which is the main Reykjavik tourist office. To the north is the Old Harbour.

Turning south from the square is the Rádhúsid (City Hall) and Tjörnin (City Pond), which are always lovely places along which to walk. Just past the pond's west bank, and slightly to the south, is the National Museum of Iceland.

GETTING AROUND

Public transport in and around the capital is by bus, and the Strætó is Reykjavik's transport system. The main termini are at Lækjartorg in the heart of the city and at Hlemmur, just to the east but still fairly central. Buses cover the whole area as well as the six neighbouring communities and comprise 35 different bus routes. They usually run from 07.00 to 24.00 (except on Sunday, when they start at 10.00). Single fares are 220Kr., half that for children, and a block of tickets costs around 1500Kr. All can be purchased from the bus driver. For more information contact ⓦ www.bus.is.

The **Reykjavik Tourist Card** includes using the Strætó for the duration of the card, as well as entry to most of the city's museums and all of its thermal pools, and is available for a 24-, 48- or 72-hour period. The tourist card can be purchased from Tourist Information Centres, Strætó bus stations, the BSI Coach Terminal and at a number of attractions and other outlets in the city, and the card costs 1200Kr. for 24 hours, 1700Kr. for 48 hours and 2200Kr. for the 72-hour version.

Taxis operate throughout the city. Though comparatively expensive, they are quick and efficient and arrive on time. All the official vehicles have meters and rates are standardised. As an example, a 5- to 10-min journey from the centre to the domestic airport will cost around 1000Kr.

Taxi companies in the city include:

Hreyfill-Bæjarleidir ☏ 588 5522 or 553 3500

BSR taxis ☏ 561 0000

Borgarbílastödin ☏ 552 2440

BSH taxis ☏ 555 0888.

CAR HIRE

After a day or two in the city, the desire to explore the country will become pretty powerful. If excursions or day tours are not the

answer, the possibilities for car hire are excellent. Iceland has several car rental companies, as well as wonderful countryside that begs to be seen. Most of the main roads are good to adequate.

A warning, however, that some of the routes that are mapped are 'F' or mountain (highland) roads. Four-wheel-drive vehicles are an absolute must for these thoroughfares, and sometimes even they are not powerful enough to deal with the conditions. Prices for rental, additional insurance and the high cost of extra petrol consumption make this option very costly although feasible. For a short break in Reykjavik, however, there are enough graded and partially graded roads to make driving, even in a conventional car, enough of an adventure.

Prices vary slightly between the companies, but generally a small economy car, collected and dropped off at Keflavik, with a 200 km (125 mile) daily limit (Iceland IS a small country) and basic insurance, will cost around 6500Kr. per day in the summer. Better deals can probably be made if booked in advance, and often the best prices are those included in a pre-booked package.

There are more than a dozen company that rent out cars in and around Reykjavik, but the major ones are:

Avis ☎ 562 3590 ⓦ www.avis.is
Budget ☎ 567 8300 ⓦ www.budget.is
Europcar ☎ 565 3800 ⓦ www.europcar.is
Hertz ☎ 505 0600 ⓦ www.hertz.is

The Pearl (page 93) offers great views over the city

Inner city & the harbour

Although Reykjavik sprawls over quite a large region, the inner city, where most things of tourist interest lie, is very small. At a sprint, the area can be covered in a couple of hours. Nevertheless, there is much to see. Several museums and art galleries are located centrally, as well as boutique and souvenir shopping. The city's history is visible here together with the distinctive brightly coloured corrugated iron houses that are identified with Reykjavik. Parks and sculptures punctuate the area.

The inner city, 101 Reykjavik, and the Old Harbour are where things are happening, and restaurants, coffee houses and clubs huddle here in a mass. These venues are often next door to each other, and a good pub crawl that lasts all night, and well into the

AN INNER CITY WALK – PART 1
Begin at Lækjartorg, the true city centre and one of the bus station terminals, and walk towards the City Pond (Tjörnin). Cross the bridge into the City Hall (Rádhúsid), stopping to look at the relief map of Iceland for general orientation. Pass by, or if there's time, even stop in to the Cathedral (Domkirkjan) and Parliament House (Althingi), on the way to Adalstræti. This area is the oldest part of the city, with Adalstræti 10 one of the city's original houses (just next door is the main Reykjavik Tourist Office). Continue through the Grofin area, past the bright yellow Kaffi Reykjavik, to the picturesque harbour. Filled with brightly coloured fishing boats, this area is a delight to visit. Heading east, return to Lækjartorg.

AN INNER CITY WALK – PART 2

Walking south on Lækjartorg, turn left at Bankastræti. Head up the hill and begin window shopping, perhaps stopping at one of the cafés for a break. Follow the street until it comes to Hlemmur, the other Stræti bus terminal. Head south on Raudarstigur until reaching the Kjarvlsstadir art museum. After the visit, meander westwards, crossing the larger street of Snorrabraut up the hill to Hallgrimskirja church. A look at the interior is a must and, on a clear day, so is a trip up to the tower to see the view. Head back into the centre via Skólavordustigur and its fine arts and crafts shops, returning to Bankastræti.

morning, may not require anything more than walking – or staggering – down the street. Buses and taxis zigzag in and out of the pedestrian zones, but are not really needed except to go to outer Reykjavik or further afield.

SIGHTS & ATTRACTIONS

Adalstræti

In the early days of Reykjavik this was the original, and for a while, only, street in the city. Full of Icelandic charm missing in other more modernised parts of the city, archaeological digs are still going on among the shops and restaurants. The city's main tourist office is here. ⓐ Adalstræti 2, Reykjavik 101 ⓣ 590 1500 ⓦ www.visitreykjavik.is

▶ *The iconic Hallgrimskirkja took nearly 40 years to construct*

Althingishúsid

Not much to look at, but historically very important, this grey basalt Parliament (Althingi) building is the national seat of government. Originally at Thingvellir since AD930, the body was disbanded when the Danish took power. In 1881, seven years after being granted self-government, the building was constructed. In 1944, Iceland became an independent nation. ⓐ 150 Reykjavik ⓣ 563 0500 ⓦ www.althingi.is

Rádhúsid (City Hall)

This modern building, constructed in 1992, successfully blends its indoor and outdoor aspects, while sitting on top of the City Pond. Open to the public, it's worth entering to see the huge relief map of Iceland as well as whatever exhibition may be on show. A coffee bar and public toilets add to its appeal. ⓐ Tjarnargotu101 ⓣ 563 2000.

Domkirkjan (Cathedral)

The Lutheran Cathedral is placed prominently on Austurvöllur Square. Built in 1848, this modest building is considered, by some, to be a work of art. Services are held here on a regular basis.
ⓐ Austurvöllur Square ⓣ 520 9700 ⓦ www.domkirkjan.is/enska.html

Hallgrimskirkja (Hallgrims Church)

The tallest and certainly most distinctive building in Reykjavik, Hallgrimskirkja resembles a rocket ship. Begun in 1949 but finished only in 1986, the interior is surprisingly peaceful considering how radical the exterior is. It's possible to ascend the 75 m/250 ft tower (at a small fee) for a spectacular view of the city.
ⓐ Skolavordustigur ⓣ 551 0745 ⓦ www.hallgrimskirkja.is

▶ *Brightly coloured fishing boats add to the ambience of the harbour*

Laekjatorg Square

Not so much an attraction but rather a point of orientation, this square is at the geographic, if not spiritual, heart of the central city. One of the city's bus terminals is here. At the top of the grassy hill is a statue of Ingolfur Arnarson, the Norwegian Viking credited with being the city's first settler (see page 14).

Laugavegur–Bankastræti–Skólavördustigur

101 Reykjavik's main shopping streets run into each other. Laugavegur is the longest, running east-west, and is full of quirky and high-fashion shops. At its western end it runs into Bankastræti, which leads to the centre of the city. At an angle to Laugavegur, leading

⬤ *Just so you don't mistake Laugavegur and its shops...*

literally up to Hallgrimskirkja, is Skólavördustigur, a street which is developing a reputation as the art (shop and gallery) avenue.

The Old Harbour

Commercially replaced by the central harbour around Sæbraut, the old harbour has been left for tourist seagoing excursions and for its charm. Tiny fishing boats are moored here, as well as what's left of the old whaling fleet. Whale- and puffin-watching trips leave from here in the season (see page 41).

Tjörnin (City pond)

Reykjavik's city 'pond' is more of a lake, a delightful rural aspect in the midst of the urban environment. Strolling along the banks offers excellent views of the city to the east, while a shooting fountain casts a rainbow over the scene on sunny days. Waterfowl linger on the shore hoping for handouts.

CULTURE

The Culture House

The jewel in this collection is the permanent display of medieval manuscripts. The well-presented vellum texts are the oldest accounts remaining of Iceland's greatest literary works, the Sagas. The other permanent and changing exhibitions have national relevance, and are usually interesting, too.

ⓐ Hverfisgata 101 ⓣ 545 1400 ⓦ www.thjodmenning.is
ⓛ Daily 11.00–17.00 ⓝ buses 1, 3, 4, 5, 6, 11, 12, 13.

Hafnarhús – Reykjavik Art Museum

Creatively recycling old port warehouses, the Art Museum's

headquarters were rehoused here in 2000. Six halls are filled with the permanent collection, including an exhibition from the Icelandic pop artist Erró. There are also changing shows from both domestic and foreign artists.

ⓐ Tryggvagata 101 ☎ 590 1200 ⓦ www.listasafnreykjavikur.is
🕒 Daily 10.00–17.00 Ⓝ buses 1, 3, 4, 5, 6, 11, 12, 13, 14, 15.

National Gallery of Iceland

Foreign and domestic painters are well represented here in a gallery that was founded in 1884. A shop and restaurant are also on the grounds.

ⓐ Fríkirkjuvegur 101 ☎ 515 9600 ⓦ www.listasafn.is
🕒 Tues–Sun 11.00–17.00 Ⓝ buses 1, 3, 4, 5, 6, 11, 12, 13, 14.

National Museum of Iceland

Completely renovated in late 2004, this state-of-the-art museum depicts the 1200 years of Iceland's social and cultural history. The displays are extremely well presented using the latest exhibition technology. A branch of the coffee house Kaffitár helps give the visitor enough stamina to get through the large exhibitions.

ⓐ Sudurgata 41 ☎ 530 2200 ⓦ www.natmus.is 🕒 Tues–Sun 10.00–18.00 (1 May–15 Sept), Tues–Sun 11.00–17.00 (16 Sept–30 Apr) Ⓝ buses 1, 3, 4, 5, 6, 11, 12, 14.

The Nordic House

The purpose of this centre is to present Nordic culture in all its forms, and to create an interchange between the relevant countries. Information on Iceland is also displayed. Entrance to the exhibition is free. ⓐ Sturlugata 5 ☎ 551 7030 ⓦ www.nordice.is
🕒 Tues–Sun 12.00–17.00 Ⓝ buses 1, 3, 4, 5, 6, 11, 12, 14.

● *Iceland's history is impressively displayed at the National Museum*

Reykjavik Museum of Photography

Sharing premises with the City Library, the Museum has several
changing exhibitions annually, both independently and in
conjunction with other organisations. Admission is free.
ⓐ Grófarhús, Tryggvagata 15 ☎ 563 1790.

Ⓦ www.ljosmyndasafnreykjavikur.is Ⓛ Mon–Fri 12.00–19.00, Sat, Sun 13.00–17.00 Ⓝ buses 1, 3, 4, 5, 6, 11, 12, 13, 14, 15.

RETAIL THERAPY

Most of 101 Reykjavik is laden with boutiques, stores, bars and restaurants, although the primary shopping streets are Laugavegur, Skólavördustígur, Bankastræti and Austurstræti.

Street markets are not really a feature in the city – the outdoor fruit and veg stalls are often health food stores advertising their slightly more expensive produce. However, the Kolaportid flea market is fun with its collection of strange secondhand items and even weirder Icelandic food items.

66° North Iceland's home-grown all-weather clothing company has as its catchphrase 'there is no bad weather – just the wrong clothing'. The expensive but well-made clothes suit the Icelandic climate perfectly.
ⓐ Lækjargata 4 Ⓣ 561 6800 Ⓦ www.66north.is
Ⓛ Mon–Fri 10.00–18.00, Sat–Sun 10.00–16.00.

Blue Lagoon Spa Shop The famous hot spring resort has a conveniently located shop in town. The cosmetics and skin care products are made from a combination of minerals, silica and algae and are supposed to be great for skin (but awful for hair!).
ⓐ Adalstræti 2 Ⓣ 517 8819 Ⓦ www.bluelagoon.is
Ⓛ Mon–Fri 10.00–18.00, Sat–Sun 10.00–14.00.

Ⓞ *In a building next to the harbour, Kolaportid is the city's flea market*

Bónus Bonus, the logo of which is 'a pink pig getting a coin rammed into its head', is a basic supermarket that provides the least expensive food shopping in Iceland. Not very good on exotic or foreign goods, but quite adequate on essential foodstuffs, this store is probably the best bet to save a few kronur.

ⓐ Laugavegur 59 101 ☎ 562 8200 ⓦ www.bonus.is
🕐 Mon–Thur 12.00–18.30, Fri 10.00–19.30, Sat 10.00–18.00.

Hans Petersen This good, general camera supply shop is well located in the centre of town. Hans Petersen is the main Kodak dealer in Iceland, and has digital supplies as well as conventional film.

ⓐ Bankastræti 4 ☎ 570 7560 ⓦ www.hanspetersen.is
🕐 Mon–Fri 10.00–18.00, Sat–Sun 10.00–16.00.

IDA English is almost as widely spoken as Icelandic here, and this modern bookshop caters to Iceland's second language extremely well. There is a large range of newspapers, postcards, gift-wrapping supplies – and even books.

ⓐ Lækjargata 2a ☎ 511 5001 ⓦ www.ida.is 🕐 Daily 09.00–22.00.

Kolaportid Reykjavik's famous harbourside flea market is located in an old port building. It's famous for offbeat items, ranging from old rock memorabilia to vintage clothing and antique books. The food section is particularly well known, selling uniquely Icelandic items such as *Hardfiskur* (dried strips of fish eaten like crisps) and *Hákarl* (rotted shark meat).

ⓐ Kolaportid (harbourside) 🕐 Sat–Sun 11.00–17.00.

Kolbrún S. Kjarval Gallery Kolbrún's ceramic work has gained international recognition and this little gallery also happens to be her studio. This shop is one of the many fine art galleries on this street.

📍 Skólavördustígur 22 101 ☎ 511 1197 🌐 www.umm.is

Mariella Mariella is the artist/jeweller who produces one-off pieces. Her speciality is to blend natural Icelandic materials such as lava and horsehair into her work.

📍 Skólavördustígur 12 ☎ 561 4500 ✉ m.mariella@bluewin.ch
🕐 Mon–Fri 11.00–18.00, Sat–Sun 10.00–16.00.

Ostabúdin Ostabúdin is probably Reykjavik's premier delicatessen and a wonderful place to view, as well as to buy. Icelandic and foreign cheeses are especially well represented. Light lunches are also served.

📍 Skólavördustígur 8 ☎ 562 2772 🌐 www.ostabudin.is
🕐 Mon–Fri 11.00–18.00, Sat–Sun 11.00–16.00.

Veidihornid Virtually all the fly-fisherman's needs can be filled at this very elegant angling and hunting shop. Most of the famous brand names are here, and the store tries to make its prices competitive with comparable shops in Europe.

📍 Hafnarstræti 5 ☎ 551 6760 🌐 www.veidhornid.is
🕐 Mon–Fri 08.00–20.00, Sat–Sun 10.00–16.00.

Vinbud The government-run off-licence has several locations throughout the city, although this one is the most centrally located. Stop here for a somewhat cheaper beer or bottle of wine and, like the Icelanders, start the drinking before going to the pub.

📍 Austurstræti 10a ☎ 562 6511 🌐 www.vinbud.is
🕐 Mon–Thur 11.00–18.00, Fri 11.00–19.00, Sat 11.00–16.00.

TAKING A BREAK

Café Paris Prominently placed in the centre of town, this is a great place to order a jug of coffee and watch the world go by. Light meals are also on the menu. ⓐ Austurstraeti 14 ⓣ 551 1020 ⓦ www.cafeparis.is ⓛ Daily from 11.00.

Kaffitár One of the more popular places to hang out and have a break, this colourful coffee house has a range of different coffee beans from around the world. There are also outlets in the National Museum and in Kringlan shopping mall. ⓐ Bankastræti 8 ⓣ 511 4540 and 588 0440 ⓦ www.kaffitar.is ⓛ Mon–Sat 07.30–18.00, Sun 10.00–17.00.

Kjarvalstadir This branch of the Reykjavik Art Museum has a spacious and pleasant restaurant, serving coffee and light meals. With views over the gardens, this is a perfect place to pause among all the art. ⓐ Flókagata 105 ⓣ 517 1290 ⓦ www.listasafnreykjavikur.is ⓛ Daily 10.00–17.00.

Sandholt A renowned bakery, this shop displays mouth-watering goodies to go with their coffee. More substantial fare is also on the menu. ⓐ Laugavegur 36 ⓣ 551 3524 ⓛ Mon–Thur 11.00–01.00, Fri–Sat 11.00–05.30, Sun 12.00–24.00.

Te og Kaffi Branches of this café can be found in various places around the country, and the central Reykjavik branch is always busy. Speciality coffees and pastries are available, as well as snack meals. ⓐ Laugavegur 24 ⓣ 562 2322 ⓦ teogkaff.is ⓛ Mon–Wed 07.30–19.00, Thur–Fri 07.30–23.00, Sat 10.00–23.00, Sun 12.00–18.00.

TAKING A DIP

Enjoying thermal pools is not just a leisure activity – it's more an Icelandic way of life. The word 'Laug', which appears regularly, including in the name of the city's premier shopping street, Laugavegur, means 'pool'. Most Reykavingurs indulge in a regular swim, and it's often the spot for some heated discussion, so to speak.

Sunhöllin A neoclassical-style pool built in 1940, this is Reykjavik's only thermal pool that's under cover. ❸ Baronstígur ❶ 551 4059 ❶ Mon–Fri 06.30–21.30, Sat–Sun 08.00–19.00 ❶ buses 14, 15, 16.

Vesturbæjarlaug Close to the Old Port, this pool is easy to walk to from anywhere in the central city. ❸ Hofsvallagata ❶ 551 5004 ❶ Mon–Fri 06.30–22.00, Sat–Sun 08.00–22.00 ❶ buses 11, 13, 15.

AFTER DARK

Many of Reykjavik's restaurants serve coffee, lunch, dinner and then change into late-night bars and clubs. Among these chameleons are:

Café Sólon £ A true Reykjavik coffee house, this is the sort of place to spend hours sipping java and chatting with friends, or people watching. On Saturday and Sunday, the late-night club can get pretty wild. ❸ Bankastræti 7a ❶ 562 3232 ❶ www.solon.is ❶ Mon–Thur 11.00–01.00, Fri–Sat 11.00–05.30, Sun 12.00–24.00.

Café Victor £ Right in the heart of the old district, Café Victor is a

good place to drink coffee, eat a snack, gorge on a substantial meal, or weekend party well into the next morning.

ⓐ Hafnarstræti 1–3 ❶ 561 9555 Ⓦ www.cafevictor.is

Vegamot £ Casual but well-attended combo venue, the food is international and the décor Mediterranean. Lots of regulars come here, and it's possible to hang out until the place turns into somewhere a bit more lively. ⓐ Vegamótastígur 4 ❶ 511 3040 Ⓦ www.vegamot.is

Apothek Bar & Grill ££ The former pharmacy (Reykjavikurapothek) has been converted to a large and elegant restaurant serving beautifully presented excellent international cuisine. Just next door is Maru, a Japanese restaurant with a sushi bias, and the two menus occasionally overlap. Apothek's bar serves a scaled-down menu, both in selection and in price, and is a very popular evening hang out. ⓐ Austurstræti 16 ❶ 575 7900 Ⓦ www.veitingar.is ❶ Mon–Thur 11.00–01.00, Fri–Sat 11.00–01.00, Sun 14.00–24.00.

The city also has several fine restaurants, offering almost any cuisine one can think of. Among those offering local dishes are:

Lækjarbrekka ££ The archetypal tourist restaurant but quite good nevertheless, Lækjarbrekka prides itself on providing national cuisine. On the menu it's possible to find reindeer, smoked lamb, Icelandic caviar, Arctic char and puffin. ⓐ Bankastræti 2 ❶ 551 4430 Ⓦ www.laekjarbrekka.is/en ❶ Daily 11.00–24.00.

◐ *While away a few hours chatting and people-watching at a coffee house*

Thrir Frakkar ££ A small restaurant slightly off the beaten track, but still in the centre, where diners nevertheless have a sense of being in on a well-guarded secret. With traditional dishes prepared in the old-fashioned way, offerings on the menu include catfish, shark and whale. ⓐ Baldursgata 14 ⓣ 552 3939 ⓦ www.3frakkar.com ⓛ Mon–Fri 11.30–14.30, 18.00–22.00; Sat–Sun 18.00–23.00.

Bars, clubs & discos

There are a tremendous number of places to hang out until the wee hours. The venues are very fluid, however, with places going in and out of business quickly, and even more fleeting is their moment of fashion. Check with the monthly listings guides (see page 37) for updates.

At weekends, when the parties happen, nothing much occurs till midnight, and then the action goes on until about 05.00 or 06.00 in the morning.

Hverfisbarinn A casual place geared more towards the younger age group, the club gets packed at weekends when there's a DJ and sometimes live music. Expect to wait in a long queue for entry after midnight. ⓐ Hverfisgata ⓣ 511 6700 ⓦ www.hverfisbarinn.is

Kaffibarinn A London underground sign welcomes the visitor to this little bar up the hill from Laugavegur. Partly owned by Blur's Damon Albarn, this place can allegedly get a bit rough late at weekends. ⓐ Bergstadarstræti 1 ⓣ 551 1588 ⓛ Daily 11.00–05.00.

Oliver At the time of writing, this is the trendiest bistro-club in Reykjavik. The restaurant does have an unofficial dress code, and the locals here can be a bit arrogant. Still, it is currently *the* place to be

seen. ⓐ Laugavegur 20a ⓣ 552 2300 ⓦ www.cafeoliver.is
ⓛ Mon–Thur 08.00–01.00, Fri 08.00–04.30, Sat 09.00–04.30,
Sun 09.00–01.00.

Pravda A bar and nightclub patronised by the younger crowd, this
place can get fairly lively at weekends. One of the trendier places to
hang out. ⓐ Austurstræti 22 ⓣ 552 9222 ⓦ www.pravda.is

Prikid Despite catering to a younger crowd, this bar is one of
Reykjavik's oldest. Located in the heart of things on Bankastræti,
food is also served here. ⓐ Bankastræti 12 ⓣ 694 5553
ⓦ www.prikid.is ⓛ Mon–Thur 07.30–01.00, Fri 07.30–05.00, Sat
12.00–05.00, Sun 12.00–01.00.

Sirkus Slightly downmarket, cheap and cheerful, this bar caters for a
younger, more alternative crowd. On some weekends there's live
music. ⓐ Klapparstíggur 31 101 ⓣ (of the owner) 864 5966.

Cinemas & Theatres
Regnboginn Cinema This multi-screen cinema shows first-run and
art-house films. It's also the sights of various film festivals. Check
monthly listings guides and the *Grapevine* newspaper for more
details. ⓐ Hverfisgata 54 ⓣ 551 9000.

National Theatre Iceland's National Theatre company performs
international and national plays, while also premiering between ten
and fourteen original pieces every year. The architecture of the
rather dour but impressive building is based on basalt columns
taken from Iceland's volcanic scenery. ⓐ Hverfisgata 19 ⓣ 551 1200
ⓦ www.leikhusid.is

Beyond the centre

Beyond the compact centre where one can find most of Reykjavik's sights, are the sprawling suburbs. At this point the capital begins to resemble an American city, rather than a European one, with fairly large distances between attractions and just a few too many miles to walk. Here public transport comes into its own, with the excellent bus service making the outer city almost as accessible as the inner. See map on pages 60–61 for the location of sights in this section.

The country reverts to its natural state quite quickly, and even within the official city limits scenery begins to overwhelm the residential development. The chain of parks that begins with Tjörnin, the pond surrounding the City Hall, begin to get closer to each other until they come together at the Ellidaár, the city's fishable salmon river. At the edges, it's hard to tell where Reykjavik ends and the countryside begins.

There are three areas of particular interest in the outer city: Laugardalur Valley, Öskjuhlíd Hill and Ellidaár Valley.

SIGHTS & ATTRACTIONS

LAUGARDALUR VALLEY

The story goes that the explorers who first spotted the site of the future capital called the area 'Reykja-vik', or 'smoky bay'. What they assumed was smoke rising from fires was actually steam from the natural hot springs that are found here. Their existence is most likely the reason that the city's biggest thermal pool was built on this spot. Surrounding it is the nation's best sporting facility and a large sports stadium, home to the Icelandic football team, as well as to most of its athletic events. Also in the area is the Asmundursafn, a branch of the Reykjavik Art Museum that features the work of Asmundur Sveinsson, the Reykjavik Park and Zoo and the Reykjavik Botanical Garden.

Laugardalur Park

This complex is where many of the city's inhabitants come to get fit and have fun. The grounds offer football fields, for both the popular and surprisingly successful Icelandic International team and the weekend player. There is also the large athletic stadium where people seriously train all year round. Other facilities include a tennis and badminton hall and a skating rink.

Probably the best thing for the visitor to do is to indulge in the geothermally heated waters and the next-door gym and spa. The Laugardalur outdoor area consists of two outdoor pools, one for serious laps and the other for splashing around. In the open-air are also four hot pots, a whirlpool and a wading pool. Inside is another competition arena for the country's professionals as well as the nation's keener amateur swimmers. The entry fees are low enough, and the opening hours amenable enough, for almost everyone to have the money and the time to come here. ⊕ Buses 2, 14, 15.

Laugar Spa

Less affordable but far more luxurious are the World Class Gym and Laugar Spa. The former is a huge state-of-the-art workout zone with hundreds of pieces of equipment designed to keep the Reykjavikingur fit and healthy. Before and after the usual business day the gym is packed. Adjoining it is the hedonistic Laugar Spa, a place designed to allow the visitor to wallow in water-based indulgences. There are several steam baths, a few with soothing lighting and subtle earth smells rising up through the mist. Some of the saunas seem to have shockingly high temperatures, which make the consequent cold showers (in the shape of waterfalls) particularly refreshing. All the usual treatments are on offer, such as mud packs and massages. There are professional medical practitioners on the staff, as well as beauticians, nutritionists, manicurists and a range of people whose aim is to make the participant feel and look well. A restaurant serving healthy food and, surprisingly, wine is hiding in the back within the spa, and it's possible to sit in a bathrobe among the candles and soft music and nibble away.

ⓐ Sundlaugavegur 30a 105 ⓣ 553 0000 ⓦ www.laugarspa.is
ⓛ Mon–Fri 06.00–23.30, Sat–Sun 08.00–20.00, gym closes half hour before. ⓝ Buses 2, 14, 15.

Reykjavik Botanical Gardens

Though open all year, these gardens are best in the summer. Featuring mostly Icelandic plants, with a few foreign species thrown in for variety, this assembly has been open since 1961. There are research projects underlying the leisure aspect – scientists are experimenting with how the flora adapts to the country's relatively harsh environment. Entry is free. ⓐ Sunnuvegur 105 ⓣ 553 8870
ⓛ Daily 10.00–22.00 Apr–Sept, 10.00–17.00 Oct–Mar

Reykjavik Family Park and Zoo

Comprising three sections, the Family Park, Zoo and Science World is an ideal place to take the kids. Open all year, there's always something going on to interest everyone.

The speciality of the Zoo is to show Icelandic animals (of which there are virtually no endemic species – most of these home-grown

ⓞ *Swim, play or just sit in one of the pools at Laugar*

● *A hot pot is just the place to recover from shopping and sightseeing*

creatures are farm animals). There are some examples of non-native wildlife which have adapted to the climactic conditions, such as foxes and reindeer. Activities for children include riding on an Icelandic Horse. The Family Park has a playground and activities. There is a café and a grill, if summer visitors want to barbecue their own hot dogs. Science World opened in 2004 and is continually growing. Featuring a touching and feeling display, active participation in the exhibitions is encouraged. The emphasis is on science and new technologies.

ⓐ Hafrafell v/Engjaveg 104 ⓣ 575 7800 ⓦ www.husdyrgardur.is
ⓛ Daily 10.00–18.00 (15 May–24 Aug), 10.00–17.00 (24 Aug–15 May)
ⓝ buses 2, 14, 15.

ÖSKJUHLÍD HILL

This area's most prominent landmark is the Pearl, visible from much of the city. Though the hill isn't that high, and it's easy enough to ascend the mound on foot, the elevation is just enough to grant great views over the rest of Reykjavik. The whole area surrounding the building is a park, with hiking and biking trails, picnic tables and even a beach.

The Pearl (Perlan)

This strange building looking like a glorified series of water tanks is, in fact, just that. Composed of six hot-water storage facilities used for heating the city, the architect covered the assembly with a glass dome, and created a major tourist attraction. Just under the dome is one of Reykjavik's best-known restaurants, with a gastronomic reputation to match. Step outside on a clear day, and the 360-degree view of the city and its surroundings is wonderful .

Also within the building are occasional exhibits and a fountain that sporadically spurts up three floors. One of the six tanks has been emptied of water and filled with the Saga Museum (see page 99), a collection of wax figures recreating the old days of Iceland.

In the grounds is another spurting fountain imitating the activities of one of the country's most famous geysers, Strokkur.
ⓐ Öskhulíd 105 ⓣ 562 0200 ⓛ daily 10.00–23.30 (observatory)
ⓦ bus 7.

Nauthólsvik Beach

Down the other side of the hill, past the airport and into the wooded area, are walking and jogging paths that lead to the sea. Here, along the sound, is a golden beach, filled with bathers on warm summer days. Built by importing sand and roping off and excluding the cold natural sea, the thermal beach was created by harnessing the city's hot water runoff from the central heating systems. The area had always been popular with warm-weather visitors until 1985, when the spot was closed. In 2000 the new facility opened and has proved very popular. Recently the beach was awarded the Blue Flag Certificate, an assurance that the place is maintaining its high-quality clean and safe environment.

Around the beach, loads of other activities are on offer. Sail and row boats and canoes can be rented, while the Siglunes Sailing Club (☎ 551 3177) gives bay tours. Bikes go whizzing past and the more energetic jog by. If all this activity is too much, Café Nautholl rests slightly back into the woods, but still grants its customers an excellent view of the proceedings from its deck while offering good coffee and light meals.

ELLIDAÁR VALLEY

Some way to the east of the centre but still within the city limits is the green valley of Ellidaár. There is a distinctly rural feeling here, helped by the salmon river running through the middle. Declared a municipal conservation area for its wildlife, it's a popular recreation spot. Within this region are Reykjavik's open-air museum, Arbærsafn, a thermal pool and Reykjavik Energy's Museum.

Salmon fishing

Once extremely popular, lately the supply of fish has declined drastically. There are worries that pollution may be affecting the river, or perhaps the number are dropping naturally. Still, it's a pleasure to wander around the banks. The fishing season runs from 15 June to 14 September and permits are available from the Angling Club of Reykjavik. 🏠 Háaleitisbraut 68 108 ☎ 568 6050 ✉ svfr@svfr.is

🔺 *The unmistakeable form of The Pearl sits on top of Öskjuhlíd Hill*

CULTURE

Arbærsafn

This town – recreated in the middle of Ellidaár's fields – is the Reykjavik City Museum's collection of historic buildings. Most of the houses come from the city, and rather than tear them down they were brought to the museum to preserve urban Icelandic heritage. There are a few remnants from the farm that used to be here, and they blend in well with the period. Residences of the rich (including one that used to be the British Embassy), as well as the poor, populate this little metropolis. Also in the grounds are examples of the endemic turf house, storage areas built half underground, with grass growing on the roof.

Guides in historic costumes pop out of the doorways, offering to explain a bit more about the social history of the period. There is also a small demonstration farm with domestic animals. Children can pet the sheep and horses. ❷ v/Kistuhyl 110 ❶ 411 6300 ❿ www.minjasafnreykjavik.is ● Daily 10.00–17.00 (June–August); guided tours only Mon, Wed, Fri 13.00 (1 Sept–31 May) ⓝ buses 5, 6, 12, 16, 25

Ásmundursafn

Ásmundur Sveinsson was a very popular native sculptor who died in 1982. Inspired by his own country, with its wild scenery and folkloric elements, he created sculpture that sprang from his national feeling. Sometimes controversial, his work changed from massive statues in the 1930s to abstract constructions made just before his death. Several of his works are also in the Kjarvalstadir.

Asmundur designed his house-cum-studio in a radical fashion, with architectural elements taken from distant sources, such as the pyramids in Egypt. He combined these influences in an extraordinary building, which now serves as the Reykjavik Art Museum's 'wing' for his work. Outside are several large pieces, providing a sculpture garden. Within are the more delicate items, including working models in several media, as well as sketches and drawings. A surprisingly nice presentation, with good work, but in some ways the building is more interesting than the art. ❷ Sigtún 105 (across from Laugardalur) ❶ 553 2155 ❿ www.listsafnreykjavikur.is ● Daily 10.00–16.00 (1 May–30 Sept), 13.00–16.00 (1 Oct–30 Apr).

Reykjavik Energy Museum

In 1899 the city lit up for the first time, and since 1921 most of Reykjavik's electricity supply has come from the power station in the Ellidaár Valley. In order to explain the workings to the public, the

⬥ Costumed guides welcome you to the historic buildings of Arbaersafn

electricity company opened up a museum in 1990. When the broader-based Municipal Energy Authority was founded in 1999, the museum changed its name – and its content – to cover all the sorts of energy involved in powering up the modern city. Now encompassing the Municipal Water and Geothermal heating works,

the Reykjavik Energy Museum goes into detail as to how the city creates its power.

Also on display are exhibits that include folk history and technical development as they pertain to energy. On the ground floor is the mostly school-visited PowerWorld, which explains a bit more about electricity. On occasions the Power Station is open to the public and tours are given.

ⓐ Ellidaár Valley ⓣ 567 9009 ⓦ www.nat.is/images/rvik_municipal_energy.htm ⓛ Sun 15.00–17.00 (1 Sept– 17 June), Tue–Sun 13.00–17.00 (18 June–30 Aug) and on prior request

Kjarvalsstadir – Reykjavik Art Museum

The nationally beloved 20th-century landscape painter Johnannes S. Kjarval is the museum's eponymous painter as well as one of its exhibitors. The modern gallery also displays other contemporary artists. The restaurant has fine views over the museum's lawns.

ⓐ Flókagata 105 ⓣ 517 1290 ⓦ www.listasafnreykjavikur.is ⓛ Daily 10.00–17.00 ⓝ buses 11, 13.

Saga Museum

Located within one of the Pearl's hot-water storage tanks that is no longer being used (see page 93), the Saga Museum tells of decisive events in Iceland's history using waxwork-like silicone figures. In an attempt to make everything as authentic as possible, the accessories are all made in the traditional way. Even the clothing is hand dyed. The guide, however, is more modern – each visitor is handed a CD player on entry. ⓐ Öskhulíd 105 ⓣ 511 1517 ⓦ www.sagamuseum.is ⓛ Daily 10.00–18.00 (1 Apr–30 Sept), 12.00–17.00 (1 Oct–31 Mar).

◐ *Ásmundur Sveinsson's home is as much an attraction as his works of art*

RETAIL THERAPY

Kringlan Reykjavik's giant mall is located about 4 km (2.4 miles) from the city centre, close to Öskhulíd Hill and about a 5–10 minute drive for most of the city's inhabitants. Comprising about 150 shops, restaurants and services, many European high street stores are represented. The mall also has a bank, food court, multi-screen cinema, post office and supermarket. ⓐ Kringlan 4-12 103 ⓣ 568 9200 ⓦ www.kringlan.is ⓛ Mon–Wed 10.00–18.30, Thur 10.00–21.00, Fri 10.00–19.00, Sat 10.00–18.00, Sun 13.00–17.00 ⓝ buses 5, 6, 16, 17, 110, 111, 112, 140 and 150.

Laugar Spa The five-star spa also has a sports shop, if a spare bathing suit or a pair of gym shorts is needed. ⓐ Sundlaugavegur 30a 105 ⓣ 553 0000 ⓦ www.laugarspa.is ⓛ Mon–Fri 06.00–23.00, Sat–Sun 08.00–20.00

Skeifan Just south of Laugardalur Valley is a shopping area known for its cheaper goods – by Icelandic standards! Located here is a wide range of outlet and bargain stores, supermarkets, and shops. ⓐ between Grensásvegur and Skeifan 103 ⓝ buses 2, 3, 5, 6, 15.

TAKING A BREAK

Arbærsafn The outdoor museum has a delightful snack bar that serves waffles along with the usual range of coffees and ice creams. ⓐ v/Kistuhyl 110 ⓣ 411 6300 ⓦ www.minjasafnreykjavik.is ⓛ Daily 10.00–17.00 (June–Aug) ⓝ buses 5, 6, 12, 16, 25.

ⓞ *The history of Iceland is revealed through waxworks at the Saga Museum*

The Pearl Although the flashier restaurant is upstairs, the simple café is fine for a rest. With luck, the view through the windows is almost as good as out on the deck (and distinctly warmer). ⓐ Öskhulíd 105 ❶ 562 0200 ⓦ www.perlan.is ❶ Daily 10.00–21.00 Ⓝ bus 7.

Café Nautholl Right next to Nautholsvik beach, this café stands back a bit from the crowds, but still allows good people watching from its deck. Good selection of light meals and excellent coffees. ⓐ Hlídarfótur, Nauthólsvegur 101 ❶ 562 9910.

Reykjavik Botanical Gardens The garden's café Floran offers a break from wandering through the flowers and shrubs. ⓐ Sunnuvegur 105 ❶ 553 8870 ❶ Daily 10.00–22.00 (Apr–Sept), 10.00–17.00 (Oct–Mar).

Kringlan's shopping mall food court is full of familiar American brands, such as Domino's, McDonald's and Subway, and even a couple of Icelandic names, such as the coffee shops Kaffiboxid and Kaffitár. The mall also has the supermarket Bonus and the hypermarket Hagkaup, if picnic goods prove a more affordable alternative. ⓐ Kringlan 4-12 103 ❶ 568 9200 ⓦ www.kringlan.is ❶ Mon–Sat 10.00–18.00, Sun 13.00–17.00 Ⓝ buses 5, 6, 16, 17, 110, 111, 112, 140 and 150.

TAKING A DIP

Arbærjarlaug Not far from the Reykjavik City Museum, and with both indoor and outdoor pools, this new spa also has a waterslide, sauna, solarium and steam bath. ⓐ Fylksivegur ❶ 510 7600

● Kringlan shopping mall is Reykjavik's biggest shopping centre

● Mon–Fri 06.50–22.30, Sat–Sun 08.00–22.00 (1 Apr–30 Sept), Mon–Fri 06.50–22.30, Sat–Sun 08.00–20.30 (1 Oct–31 Mar) ● buses 5, 25.

Laugardalslaug Within the Laugardal Valley sport area, these outdoor and indoor pools are Reykjavik's largest. Practise laps with the professionals, or just chat with the locals. ● Laugardalur
● 553 4039 ● Mon–Fri 06.50–21.30, Sat–Sun 08.00–20.00.

AFTER DARK

Virtually all of Reykjavik's after-dark action happens in the centre of town. The suburbs are very quiet.

Restaurants

Kringlan £–££ This has several restaurants, some of which remain operational after the shopping mall's closing time. Try the à la carte family restaurant Kringlukráin for casual dining. ⓐ Kringlan 4-12 103 ⓣ 568 0878 ⓦ www.kringlukrain.is

Perlan ££ The Pearl's top-floor revolving restaurant, open evenings only, has a top reputation which is not always warranted. Still, the venue is superb, with a magnificent view over Reykjavik. The menu is international, with an occasional Icelandic speciality, such as Arctic char on the fish menu. ⓐ Öskjuhlíð 105 ⓣ 562 0200 ⓦ www.perlan.is ⓛ Daily from 18.30

Cinemas & theatres

City Theatre Just next door to Kringlan, this repertory theatre has four stages on which there are at least seven major projects annually, as well as several other smaller productions. The venue's programme includes everything from rock concerts to philosophical debates. ⓐ Listabraut 3 103 ⓣ 568 8000 ⓦ www.borgarleikhus.is

Sambio Kringlan's cinema shows all the latest Hollywood films, some even before they've arrived in the UK. ⓐ Kringlan ⓦ www.kvikmyndir.is

---

● *If you are travelling away from the city, a visit to Geysir is a must*

The Blue Lagoon & the Reykjanes Peninsula

Only about 50 km (31 miles) away from Reykjavik, and one of Iceland's biggest tourist attractions, is the Blue Lagoon. A huge pool brimming with the heated overspill from the nearby power plant, this enormous outdoor spa is supposed to be excellent for healing skin complaints and other ailments. Although possibly a day's activity in its own right, there are also many other things to see in the area.

Keflavik, nearby and better known for being the site of the international airport, offers whale watching in the season. Grindavik is a small fishing village with a museum that pays tribute to what was once the country's biggest money earner, Icelandic *Saltish* (salt cod). Further away, on some roads that might qualify as a driving adventure, are the dramatic cliffs of Krisuviksberg. Not far from here is Seltun, sight of a once energetic geysir, now a weird area of thermal pools and bubbling mud. Just before heading back to Reykjavik is Hafnarfjödur with its 'hidden' residents.

SIGHTS & ATTRACTIONS

The Blue Lagoon

On the way into Reykjavik from Keflavik International Airport, what looks like billowing white smoke rises above the fields of black lava. This plume is actually steam, and it comes from the nearby power station. Just next to it is the Blue Lagoon, the pool that gets its water from the plant. Many visitors stop en route to or from the airport to take a dip, and some tour operators' pick-up services include some time here.

The Blue Lagoon is an artificial pool created when hot seawater

was pumped out from the geothermally fuelled Svartsengi power plant, creating a lagoon. Running over the lava fields, the minerals within some of the water crystallised. Icelanders, being the thermal spa lovers that they are, started bathing in the pond. Psoriasis sufferers began to notice improvements in their skin when they rubbed some of the grainy white sludge onto the affected areas. In 1987 this therapy was acknowledged, and the first public pool opened. Gradually more facilities, such as medical staff, geothermal spa and massages became part of the spa. Now what once seemed to be mud is packaged as a skin product, sold at fine shops and sent all over the world. The spa has never been more popular.

The milky-turquoise blue water spreads over a huge area,

surrounded by dark lava hills. Steam pumped from the centre of the pool rises up and, in the distance, a matching column rises from the source, the out-of-view power station. Within the lagoon are roped-off areas creating separate pools, as well as an energetic waterfall under which visitors can stand. Just next to them is a steam bath in what looks like a cave in the lava. Just beyond is a shallower pool where people can smear the white, healing mud all over their faces.

The place is incredibly popular with both locals and visitors and is advertised as one of the major tourist attractions of Iceland. Few, if any other, spas claim that their constituent parts are so good for

---

The milky water at the Blue Lagoon is reputed to have healing properties

the skin, and the Blue Lagoon's products are certainly hyped. Though a lot of fun, and extremely photogenic, the place does get a bit crowded at times. Being there at peak times can feel like taking a bath at a rail station in rush hour. Entry fees are reasonable.

The Blue Lagoon is 16 km (10 miles) away from Keflavík and 48 km (30 miles) from Reykjavík. It takes approximately 20 minutes to drive from the airport. Airport taxis offer special deals to stop at the lagoon to or from Reykjavik, and the airport transfer bus will make a stop for passengers arriving between 15.00 and 16.00. Thingvallaeid bus company has six departures daily and offers a package that includes the Blue Lagoon's entry fee. Tours leave regularly from most hotels and guesthouses.

ⓐ 240 Grindavik ❶ 420 8800 ⓦ www.bluelagoon.com ❶ Daily 09.00–21.00 (15 May–31 Aug), 10.00–20.00 (1 Sept–14 May).

Gardskagi

At the northern tip of the Reykjanes Peninsula is the lighthouse at Gardskagi. Close to the town of Gardur, there has been a beacon here since 1847, when a lamp was put on the top of a sign. A subsequent tower was built in 1897, but the one that's there now dates from 1944. During the migration periods of April–May and September–October, birdwatching 'twitchers' have a literal field day. To drive there, take route 41 west from Reykjavik. Just beyond Keflavik, turn north on route 45. ⓦ www.nat.is

Grindavik

This seaside village is the Blue Lagoon's closest urban access. Though one of Iceland's most important fishing ports, tourism is beginning to play an important role and the town does have a few attractions in its own right. There are coastal walks as well as

ELVES

With a rich folklore that goes all the way back to the settlement of the country in the 9th century, elves, trolls and ghosts pervaded the Icelandic psyche. Now, with the interest in trolls receding, and electric light causing the demise of ghosts, elves remain a part of most Icelanders' lives. When questioned, locals may not vocalise their belief, but will admit that they wouldn't do anything to upset an elf. Documented cases exist of road builders who claim that when they moved a rock that was alleged to be an elf's home, all sorts of things went wrong. When they replaced it, suddenly everything was fine again.

Also known as the 'Hidden Folk', not many people are able to see the creatures. There are, however, acknowledged locations of their whereabouts, and Reykjavik's next-door neighbour, Hafnarfjördur, is supposed to be the home to the Royal Family of Elves. Apparently, the creatures show themselves only to those with second sight. 'Hidden Folk' do not live solely in the suburbs, however. Whenever anything disappears, or reappears in a strange place, especially after a long time, the Icelanders credit this as being of an elf's making. Interestingly enough, odd things keep on happening throughout the country...

opportunities to path-find through the lava fields. For more organised sport, there's a 9-hole golf course. The Icelandic Saltfish Museum (see page 114) is Grindavik's tribute to the industry that put so many kronur into its pockets. To get there by car, take Route 41 west till route 43, then go south. ⓦ www.grindavik.is

Hafnarfjördur

Reykjavik's next-door neighbour, barely 10 km (6 miles) away, is the 'town in the lava'. Although most of the activity is on the flat around the bay, the hills are constructed of the outflow from once active volcanoes.

One of the highlights of the town is to see the charming, brightly coloured corrugated houses that have been built within the black lava field. The harbour is lively and active, both small fishing craft and larger vessels moor here, and whale watching trips leave from this area. Also nearby is the Ástjörn Nature Reserve, a haven for both walkers and birdwatchers (at the right time of year).

The quirkiest aspect of Hafnarfjördur is its reputation for having more 'hidden folk' or mythical creatures than any other area in the country. This arguable title is due mostly to the city's best known resident, the clairvoyant Erla Stéffansdóttir. Gifted with second sight, she offers tours to where the elves live. Alternatively, a map to these stars' homes is available at the tourist office.

Hafnarfjördur Tourist Office ⓐ Strandgata 6 220 Hafnarfjordur ⓣ 585 5500 ⓦ www.hafnarfjordur.is

Krisuvik

Roads in this area are generally paved, but occasionally, and without warning, they turn into graded tracks. While rough, it is possible for an ordinary car to do the trip.

So while not far in kilometres, the way to the thermal area of Krisuvik-Seltun can be a bit of a journey. However, it's worth it to see these hissing waters and bubbling mud pools. By car, get to Grindavik then head east on route 427. When it intersects route 42, head north. For an easier journey back to Reykjavik, continue north on this road till it gets to route 41 at Hafnarfjördur.

○ *Tread carefully near the boiling water and mud of Krisuvik-Seltun*

Krisuviksberg

This dramatic headland over the sea might require a bit of effort to reach, but it's definitely worth it. The cliff rises steeply over the sea, with a sweep straight down to the blue water below. The contrast against the dark sand is dramatic. In the summer, nesting birds crowd the place. From Grindavik, continue east on 427.

CULTURE

Gardur Folk Museum

Within the lighthouse at the end of the peninsula, this little museum explains a bit about the folklore of the area

ⓐ Gardskagi Lighthouse, 250 Gardur. ✆ 422 7220 and 894 2135

🕐 Daily 13.00–17.00 (1 May–31 Aug) or upon request.

Hafnarfjördur Museum

Three historic houses make up this museum. One of the three houses, Pakkhúsid, has exhibits that tell the history of the town since Viking days plus a toy collection. The Sivertsen House depicts the life of an upper-class 19th-century family, while Siggubær is an example of a working-class home from the early 20th century.
🚉 Vestergata 8 ☎ 585 5780 🌐 www.hafnarfjordur.is/byggdasafn
🕐 Pakkhúsid: daily 11.00–17.00 (1 June–31 Aug), Sat–Sun only in winter; Sivertsen House and Siggubær: daily 11.00–1700 (1 June–31 Aug), winter by appointment.

Hidden Worlds Tour

A little offbeat, but culture of sorts, Hafnarfjördur's clairvoyant Erla Stefánsdóttir takes visitors on a tour of where the resident elves live. ☎ 694 2785 🕐 Tues, Fri 14.30 (1 Jan–15 Sept) 🌐 www.alfar.is

Icelandic Saltfish Museum

For a long time, producing saltfish (salted cod) was the biggest business in Iceland. This museum depicts the history and importance of the industry and shows how the export of this product proved to be the financial foundation of modern Iceland.
🚉 Hafnargata 12a Grindavik ☎ 420 1190 🌐 www.randburg.com/is/icelandic-saltfish-museum 🕐 Daily 11.00–18.00.

RETAIL THERAPY

Iceland's third-biggest city, Hafnarfjördur, has several stores.

Fjödur Shopping Centre comprises just about everything, including fashion, toy, camera and jewellery stores, a bank, optician and

supermarket. There are even ship brokers and accountants.
🅐 Fjardargata 13-15220 Hafnarfjördur 🅣 565 5666 or 898 5866
🅛 Mon–Thur 10.00–18.00, Fri 10.00–19.00, Sat 10.00–16.00.

Blue Lagoon shop Buy the same products that you wallow in, just inside the main building. See page 106.

TAKING A BREAK

Café Aroma Here is a place to drop your shopping bags, rest a bit and grab some caffeine. 🅐 Fjördur shopping centre IS-220 Hafnarfjördur 🅣 555 6996.

Fjörukráin Close to the tourist office is another good spot just to chill a bit 🅐 Strandgata 55 IS-220 Hafnarfjördur 🅣 565 1213.

Blue Lagoon The basic café here offers *pylsur* (hot dogs) and chips, as well as coffee. 🅐 240 Grindavik 🅣 420 8800 🅦 www.bluelagoon.com
🅛 Daily 09.00–21.00 (15 May–31 Aug), 10.00–20.00 (1 Sept–14 May).

TAKING A DIP

Blue Lagoon For the biggest thermal pool of them all, see page 106.

Gardur Swimming Centre A good place to soak away the exhaustion of a long day's touring 🅐 Gardbraut 250, Gardur 🅣 422 7300
🅛 Mon–Fri 07.00–21.00, Sat–Sun 10.00–16.00 (May–Aug).

Keflavík Swimming Centre Close to the airport one can find a 25 m pool as well as the usual hot pots and steam bath.

❷ By Sunnubraut – 230 Reykjanesbær **❶** 421 1500 **◐** Mon–Fri 06.45–21.00, Sat 08.00–17.00, Sun 09.00–16.00 (May–Aug).

Sundhöll Hafnarfjardar The pool is indoors, but the hot pots are outdoors. Linger in the sauna, too. **❷** Herjólfsgata 10, Hafnarfjödur **❶** 555 0088 **◐** Mon–Fri 06.30–21.00, Sat–Sun 08.00–12.00. Women's night: Tues, Thur 20.00–21.00.

Sudurbæjarlaug The outside pool is only part of the complex, with Nautilus gym, solarium and massages, as well as the ubiquitous hot pots and steam bath. **❷** Hringbraut 77, Hafnarfjödur **❶** 565 3080 **◐** Mon–Fri 06.30–21.30, Sat 08.00–18.30, Sun 08.00–17.30.

AFTER DARK

Restaurants
A. Hansen ££ A fine restaurant with seafood specialities and prices that are somewhat lower than Reykjavik. **❷** Vesturgata 4, 220 Hafnarfjördur **❶** 565 1130 **Ⓦ** www.ahansen.is

Blue Lagoon ££ The spa resort has an excellent restaurant with an international menu, where you can eat while watching the bathers. **❷** 240 Grindavik **❶** 420 8806 **Ⓦ** www.bluelagoon.com **◐** Daily 09.00–21.00 (15 May–31 Aug), 10.00–20.00 (1 Sept–14 May)

Grindavik has a couple of pizza places that are open in the evenings:

Cactus restaurant and bar £ **❷** Hafnargotu 6. Grindavik **❶** 426 9999 **◐** Mon–Thur 11.30–24.00, Fri–Sat 14.00–03.00, Sun 14.00–24.00 (kitchen closes 21:30) summer; Mon–Thur 18.00–24.00, Fri 18.00–

03.00, Sat 14.00–03.00, Sun 14.00–24.00 winter (kitchen closes 21.00)

Mamma mía pizzahouse £ ⊜ Víkurbraut 31, Grindavik ❶ 426 7860
🕒 Daily 12.00–22.00

ACCOMMODATION

Fiskanes Guesthouse £ Basic rooms available at reasonable prices, open 1 Apr-1 Sept only. ⊜ Hafnargotu 17-19 Grindavik ❶ 897 6388.

Fit Hostel £ Near the international airport, this youth hostel has newly renovated sleeping, cooking and bathing facilities, including a hot tub. ⊜ Fitjabraut 6A/6B, 260 Njardvik ❶ 421 8889.

Hotel Keflavik £££ This four-star hotel is a good place to stay for luxurious accommodation. ⊜ Vatnsnesvegur 12-14 Reykjanesbaer ❶ 420 7000 Ⓦ www.kef.is

Hotel Northern Light Inn £££ The closest place to stay to the Blue Lagoon, the hotel offers comfortable accommodation with all facilities. ⊜ Blue Lagoon Svartsengi 240 Grindavik ❶ 426 8650.

Camping
There are campsites in the area at:
Keflavik airport Motel rooms and sleeping-bag accommodation are also available ❶ 421 2800 Ⓦ www.alex.is
Stekkur Camping ⊜ Reykjanesbær
Vogar Camping ⊜ Vogar ❶ 424 6545 ⊜ afgreidsla@vogar.is
Grindavík Camping ⊜ Grindavík ❶ 420 1190 ⊜ kjartan@saltfisksetur.is
Gardur Camping ⊜ Gardur ❶ 422 7108 Ⓦ www.sv-gardur.is

The Golden Circle

Probably the most popular and certainly the most attended day excursion out of Reykjavik is the Golden Circle. This tour is a sort of taster of Iceland, offering a view of many of the country's varied landscapes within a relatively short period of time. It is also possible to do the trip independently, as all the roads are on paved or well-graded roads. The return trip is around 250 km (155 miles).

The first stop is Thingvellir, the site of the world's first Parliament in AD930 as well as the Great Atlantic Rift. From there the standard tour continues to Geysir, the original shooting hot spring that gave its name to similar phenomena around the world. The scenery changes suddenly as volcanic lava takes over. Visible by its rising mist long before it comes into view, the magnificent waterfall Gullfoss plunges down a deep chasm, one of Iceland's most memorable sites. On extended tours, there's a chance to pass the falls on a 4WD track to get to the glacier Langjökull and do some skidooing on the snow.

Thingvellir

A designated national park and point of national reverence as well as UNESCO Heritage Site, Thingvellir is an eerie and extraordinary place. The first view coming from the west and south is from the Visitors' Centre perched on a hill over the site. Looking down into a large depression, a lake is visible to the south (Thingvallvatn). In the far distance is a large wall rising up, matched by the one on which the visitor centre stands. In the middle is a meadow area with rivers running through and a few interesting-looking buildings with pointed roofs. Jagged lines of rock zigzag through the area.

This area is the location of the Great Atlantic Rift, the point on the planet where the North American and Eurasian tectonic plates are separating. Essentially, this is where Europe and America come together, although their meeting point is dividing at a rate of 2 cm a year. The large valley below, between the walls, is new earth, growing larger every day and is considered by some to be 'no man's land', an area of neither one continent nor the other. Some locals feel that this new land should be an area of independent government, but Icelandic officials have incorporated this spot as one of national importance.

Thingvellir is also the site that the Vikings selected for their Althing in AD930, the general assembly and the first one in recorded history. Equally accessible from most of the settlements of the period, the local chiefs came here to settle their arguments. Stories fly about the behaviour of these Nordic lords, ranging from how they resolved their disputes by duels to how they settled their differences by bribery. Apparently, bad behaviour by women was not tolerated; there is a legendary spot in the extremely cold glacial run-off river where wayward females were quickly dealt with, whether by drowning or freezing, as punishment. More documented is the location of the actual assembly, the Law Rock (Lögberg), where natural acoustics allowed whoever was speaking to be heard. Nothing remains of the original assembly, but the spot is commemorated by a flag, flying next to the church (a 1907 reconstruction of the original built in AD1000).

Also on the site is Thinvallabær, the summer residence of the country's president in the form of a traditional farmhouse, built for the 1000-year anniversary of the foundation of the Althing.

Geysir

In a delightful region of farmland and summer green fields, the land suddenly turns red and the whiff of rotten eggs is noticeable. Also apparent are the tour buses and advertisements for the café and hotel. Out of nowhere, steam seems to rise out of the earth and, if

the timing is right, a huge column of water spurts up into the sky.

Geysir is the name of one of the geysers in this small but impressive hot spring area. Erupting only after an earthquake (the last one in 2000), the plumes are supposed to reach up to 80 m (262 ft). Still, its next-door neighbour, the little but more reliable Strokkur, is pretty much why people continue to flock to this tourist attraction and natural wonder. At intervals of about 5 minutes, the geyser regularly shoots up 25–30 m (70–100 ft) into the air. The process, and anticipation, are fascinating. After an eruption, the water starts draining slowly back into the geyser's basin, rising and falling like breathing. It threatens to blow, then pulls the water back several times, the number depending on how high the last eruption was. Finally, a turquoise-blue bubble forms on the surface and suddenly hot water shoots high into the air. Sometimes there are a few little explosions surrounding the big one, although each expulsion is different. The perimeter of Strokkur is marked off, and puddles indicate which way the wind is blowing. Stay out of this area to avoid getting soaked, even though the warm water is pleasant (until it grows cold!).

Other smaller springs bubble away, and it's possible to walk around or up the hill to get a good view. Despite the ease of access and the general friendly tone, extreme caution must be exercised here. The water is hot and the earth thin, and it's possible to break through it into boiling water. Stick to the designated paths, even if it's tempting to wander outside of these borders. There is no admission charge to the thermal area. Across the street is a tourist complex, with café, hotel and other facilities. There is also a folk museum and a multi-media show on the geology of the region.

▶ *The geyser at Geysir puts on a show every 5 minutes or so*

Gullfoss

The land becomes barren and volcanic, and just about 10 km (6 miles) further northwest of Geysir, what seems to be fog rises out of the black land. In contrast to Geysir, almost nothing is visible and a small sign points to a parking area for Gullfoss. Arguably Iceland's prettiest waterfall, these incredible chutes have several viewpoints, all dramatic in their own right. Past the low-key café and shop, a path leads to an overview. In sunshine, a huge rainbow hangs over the water, a product of wind blowing the spray. The arc moves as the angle of the sun shifts.

On overcast days, the falls are still extraordinary, and the raw sense of power seems to come through more clearly. Walking down the steps, it's possible to stroll along the west bank of the Hvita River and its 2.5 km (1.5 miles) canyon towards the main falls. The lower cascade drops about 22 m (72 ft) and the upper 11 m (35 ft), but it's not the height that's impressive – rather the shape of the canyon and the amount of water pushing through. The trail leads to rocks that jut out between the two sections, and it's worth looking back along the main drop to get an impression of the sheer volume of water. A further path goes up the hill away from the falls, but grants a good overview of the area.

Langjökull Glacier

Langjökull is the country's second-largest ice field (after Vatnajökull in the east). With an area of around 950 sq. km (590 miles), its elevation varies between 1200 and 1500 m (4000 and 5500 ft). The glacier is 4WD accessible from mountain (F) tracks. The road that continues from Gullfoss is probably the easiest way to get there,

---

▶ *The views over the falls at Gullfoss are breathtaking*

although extreme caution is advised. It's strongly advised that you visit the glacier only with an organised tour as the locals know the best access points and are aware of the latest weather conditions. Glaciers are extremely dangerous, especially in falling snow, which happens at any time of the year. Light drifts cover up fragile crevasses and deep water holes, and even the most powerful vehicles can get stuck.

Nonetheless, a visit to Langjökull on a tour, often en route from the Golden Circle, is a lot of fun. Many companies, including Activity Group (ⓦ www.activity.is), Discover the World, (ⓦ www.dtw.is), Iceland Excursions (ⓦ www.icelandexcursions.is) and Mountain Taxi (ⓦ www.mountaintaxi.is), offer superjeep expeditions on the glacier. Some include snowmobiles or skidoos as part of the tour. Not quite as easy as they look but still fine for first-timers, gliding along on the glaciers via one of these modified motorbikes is great to try. It's certainly the best way to see as much as possible in the time allotted. The tours are carefully escorted and, within the framework of adventure tourism, relatively safe.

CULTURE

Geysir Centre at Geysir

Across the street from the thermal area is the complex that includes the Geysirstofa, a multi-media show that has a changing programme of Iceland's natural phenomena. Also here is an earthquake simulator, and a folk museum on the upper floors.
ⓐ Selfoss 801 ❶ 480 6800 ⓦ www.geysircenter.com
🕒 Daily 10.00–19.00 (May–Sept) 11.00–17.00 (Oct), 12.00–16.00 (Nov–Feb), 12.00–17.00 (Mar), 11.00–17.00 (Apr).

⏺ *Thingvellir is the scenic home of the first parliament*

Nesjavellir

En route to Thingvellir, stop off and take a tour of Iceland's biggest energy plant. Using only geothermal resources, the plant produces 90 MWe of electricity, giving credence to the statistic that 70 per cent of the nation's power is produced this way. ⓐ Nesjavellir ⓣ 480 2408 ⓦ www.or.is ⓛ Mon–Sat 09.00–12.00, 13.00–17.00 Sun 13.00–18.00, summer; Mon–Sat on request, winter.

Thingvellir Visitors' Centre

The first place to go when visiting the site, the visitor centre has displays, a 3D relief map and probably the best overlook of the national park. ⓐ 801 Selfoss ⓣ 482 2660 ⓦ www.thingvellir.is ⓛ Daily 08.00–20.00 (summer), Mon–Fri 09.00–17.00 (winter).

RETAIL THERAPY

Geysir Centre A surprisingly comprehensive souvenir store exists in this tourist facility, in case there's still something needed after shopping in Reykjavik. It's also possible to buy edibles for a picnic lunch in the nearby snack shop. ⓐ Selfoss 801 ① 480 6800 ⓦ www.geysircenter.com ⓛ Daily 10.00–19.00 (May–Sept), 11.00–17.00 (Oct), 12.00–16.00 (Nov–Feb) 12.00–17.00 (Mar), 11.00–17.00 (Apr).

Gullfoss Overlooking the falls is a fairly well supplied shop that sells the usual tourist goods. ⓐ Gullfoss.

Selfoss, Just south of the Golden Circle and usually on the way back to Reykjavik on Route 1 is Selfoss. The largest town in the area, with a population of over 7000, it has a large range of facilities, including a Bonus supermarket. ⓐ Austurvegur 42.

TAKING A BREAK

Geysir Centre The snack shop has standard fare, including hamburgers, chips, pizza and hotdogs and ordinary coffee. ⓐ Selfoss 801 ① 480 6800 ⓦ www.geysircenter.com ⓛ Daily 10.00–19.00 (May–Sept) 11.00–17.00 (Oct), 12.00–16.00 (Nov–Feb) 12.00–17.00 (Mar), 11.00–17.00 (Apr).

Gullfoss Getting out of the spray that pervades the area, the restaurant here is pretty decent. The Icelandic lamb stew is particularly satisfying on a cold wet day (with one free refill included). When the sky is clear, the outdoor deck is a great sun trap. ⓐ Gullfoss.

Selfoss

There are several cafés here, including:

HM café ❷ Eyrarvegur 15, ❶ 482 3535
Kaffi Krus ❷ Austurvegur 7 ❶ 482 1672
The Viking Restaurant ❷ Efstaland, Ölfus.

TAKING A DIP

Hotel Geysir The hotel across from the thermal area has a 17.5 m (60 ft) swimming pool open to the public in the summer. The adjoining hot tubs are open all year round. ❷ Haukadalur IS-801 Sellfoss ❶ 480 6800 ❿ www.geysircenter.com/english/hotel ❶ swimming pool 15 Apr–1 Sept, hot tubs all year.

Hotel Gullfoss The hotel has a hot tub on the deck for its guests. ❷ Brattholt Blaskogabyggd 801 Selfoss ❶ 486 8979 ❿ www.hotelgullfoss.is

Laugarvatn Swimming Pool On the road between Thingvellir and Geysir is the thermal resort town of Laugarvatn. Steam seems to come from everywhere, and it's possible to indulge in it, via the 25 m (80 ft) swimming pool and its two hot pots. ❷ 840 Laugarvatn ❶ 486 1251 ❿ www.nat.is

Selfoss The swimming pool is designed for the whole family. There's also a sauna. ❷ Bankavegur 800 Selfoss ❶ 482 1227 ❿ www.selfoss.is ❶ Mon–Fri 06.45–21.15, Sat–Sun 10.00–20.00, Sat 08.00–20.00 winter.

AFTER DARK

Not much goes on in the countryside outside of the hotels.
Hotel Geysir £ Right across from the geysers, this restaurant offers an international menu with the occasional Icelandic speciality, such as salt cod (*bacalao*) and guillemot. At night, the tables are candlelit.
ⓐ Selfoss 801 ⓣ 480 6800 ⓦ www.geysircenter.com

Hotel Gullfoss £ Native cuisine is prepared country-style at the in-house restaurant but more than that, it's convenient for the nearby attractions. See page 129 for contact details.

Riverside Restaurant ££ at Hotel Selfoss. One of the best venues in the area, the restaurant serves creative versions of some classic dishes. There is also a daily fixed-price menu. See page 129 for contact details.

ACCOMMODATION

Hostels & hotels

Arnes £ This youth hostel is about 22 km (13 miles) northeast of Selfoss, and well situated for what there is to see in the vicinity. A swimming pool and restaurant are nearby. In the summer there are regular bus connections to Reykjavik. ⓐ Gnúpverjahreppur, Selfoss 801. From Selfoss, go east on Route 30, then north on route 32 approximately 14 km. ⓣ 486 6048 ⓦ www.hihostels.com

Hotel Geysir £ without facilities, **££** en suite. The Geysir Centre has a range of sleeping options, with luxury cabins, rooms and even sleeping-bag accommodation, each with prices to match.
ⓐ Selfoss 801 ⓣ 480 6800 ⓦ www.geysircenter.com

Laugarvatn £ Located in the village, this youth hostel has rooms ranging from a single to a six-person capacity. Within the residence is a kitchen and TV, and just outside is a hot tub. The town's post office, bank and grocery store are close. ➋ Dalsel Laugarvatn 840 ➊ 486 1215 Ⓦ www.hihostels.com

Hotel Gullfoss ££ summer, **£** winter. This friendly hotel in a very quiet rural location has 16 rooms with full facilities ➋ at Brattholt, Bláskógarbyggd, 801 Selfoss ➊ 486 8979 Ⓦ www.hotelgullfoss.is

Hotel Selfoss ££ A luxury hotel with everything a four-star lodging should have, and it's picturesquely located right next to the same roaring river that falls through Gullfoss upstream. ➋ Hótel Selfoss, Eyrarvegi 2, 800 Selfoss ➊ 480 2500 Ⓦ www.hotelselfoss.is

Campsites
There are lots of campsites in the area. The closest ones to Golden Circle attractions are:

Hotel Geysir Along with all the other services, the Hotel Geysir even has a campsite. Get up really early in the morning and watch Strokkur erupt without anyone else around. ➋ Selfoss 801 ➊ 480 6800 Ⓦ www.geysircenter.com

Thingvellir National Park Camping Ground Two areas in the park allow camping. At Leirar just a five-minute walk from the Information Centre, there are four different sites, Fagrabrekka, Sydri-Leirar, Hvannabrekka and Nyrdri-Leirar. Further away, at Lake Thingvallavatn, is Vatnskot. Ask at the Information Centre for details and permits. ➋ 801 Selfoss ➊ 482 2660 Ⓦ www.thingvellir.is

Snaefellsnes Peninsula

On a clear day, looking northwest across the bay from Reykjavik, it's possible to make out the far distant image of a picture-perfect volcano. Rising up in a classic shape, covered with a white crown all year round, this mountain is topped by its glacier. Jules Verne used this location as the entrance to his *Journey to the Centre of the Earth,* and New Agers believe it is one of the earth's most powerful energy points.

The peak is about 200 km (125 miles) away by car from the capital, and rests at the end of another of Iceland's beautiful and easily accessible peninsulas. Within the jurisdiction of a national park, the massif and its glacier are reached either via an organised tour (see Arnarstapi, below) or independently (see Snæfellsjökull, page 133). Nearby are lovely – and sometimes lava-blackened – sea-swept beaches. To the north is the charming fishing village of Stykkishólmur and, further west, the commercial port of Olafsvik. The local waters here are yet another stomping ground for visiting sea mammals, including their largest representative, the Blue Whale. Scattered among the fields, sometimes for no apparent reason, are little churches, particularly prominent against the sweeping mountain backdrop. Most of these are open and can be entered, and if not, the local farm resident usually has the key.

SIGHTS & ATTRACTIONS

Arnarstapi
This small fishing hamlet nestles comfortably under Snæfellsjökull mountain, from which it gains its most important source of income.

● *Don't let the name of 'Garbage Bay' stop you visiting Dritvik*

Snowmobile and skidoo tours up to the glacier are offered from here, when there is enough snow on which to play (🅦 www.snofell.is). When there isn't, a four-wheel-drive road through to Olafsvik, on the north side of the peninsula, passes by its toe. Again, extreme caution is advised when venturing onto the ice. The 8 km (5 mile) walk to the next village of Hellnar, hiking through the lava fields along the rugged coast, is not as daunting as it sounds, and a pleasure on a long summer evening.

Several species of seabird overwhelm the area in the season, and a large Arctic tern colony is resident in the village. During nesting times the birds are everywhere, but pay due attention to their cautionary cries, as they can attack if they feel their chicks are threatened.

Búdir

Just off the junction of roads 54 and 574, this beautiful tidal estuary, with its golden beach, rests at the end of an impressive lava field. Only a little church and a small hotel are here. Nevertheless, the 19th-century church is charming, in a traditional wooden style, and the accommodation absolutely first class.

This is a delightful spot to get away from most of civilisation, enjoying the sea air and mountain views, while still wallowing in the luxury of an excellent resort.

Djúpalónssasndur and Dritvík

Now part of Snæfellsjökull National Park, Djúpalónssandur was once a thriving fishing port. The only reminders that this place was ever anything other than an empty beach are a few pieces of rusty metal strewn among the black stones. These remnants are the nautical equivalent of dried bleached bones, from shipwrecks of the past. A bit further along, past four increasingly large stones, the lifting of which is said to measure strength, is Dritvik ('Garbage Bay') a lovely horseshoe bay with a dark beach. The pebbles here are shiny and have been rounded by the sea, and are known as black pearls by the locals.

Olafsvik

The largest fishing port on the peninsula, this harbour has been operating as a going concern since its foundation in the 17th century. To the tourist, its prime interest is as a whale-watching centre, with boats going out to view its biggest draw – literally – the huge Blue Whale, the largest mammal on earth (Ⓦ www.seatours.is). The Old Warehouse, dating from 1844, now houses the folk museum.

Snæfellsjökull

On clear days, this magnificent mountain can be visible for hundreds of kilometres. With a height of only 1446 metres (4744 ft), and a glacier only a fraction of the size of the country's larger ice fields, this mountain nevertheless has special significance to Icelanders. Believed to be mystical by both locals and New Age travellers, the archetypal cone was briefly believed to be a landing site for extraterrestrials (who never appeared). Even Jules Verne imagined the indentation at the top to be the entrance to the planet's core, inspiring his 1864 novel, *Journey to the Centre of the Earth*. Whether more empowered than any other of Iceland's magical sites or not, the geography of the area is stunning. Rising from the sea and providing a striking backdrop to almost anywhere in Snæfellsness, it's not surprising that magical powers have been attributed to this area.

The summit of the *jökull* (glacier) can be reached on foot, via

three routes. The F (mountain) 570 runs from north to south, from Olafsvik to Arnarstapi, and passes close to the base of the ice. With a four-wheel-drive vehicle, the road can usually be reached from either town, although snow can block the pass.

There are two tracks off this route that lead to the top. The other way up leaves from the tiny fishing village of Hellisandur to the northwest of the peninsula following the 574 ring road. There is an unnamed four-wheel-drive track about 4 km (2.4 miles) inland that heads east then south towards the mountain. At the end of the road, the path heads up, eventually reaching the ice, then the peak. Glacier hiking can be very dangerous, and unless hikers are extremely experienced and knowledgeable about crossing these surfaces, a better alternative might be to take a snowmobile tour from Arnarstapi (see page 132).

Stykkishólmur

Snæfellsness's 'capital' is a delightful fishing town with a population of about 1200. Corrugated iron buildings of various colours nestle against a lively harbour, which is backed up against a lighthouse-topped cliff. The view from the top of the crag to the south overlooks the harbour and the mountains, and, to the north, the Breidalfjördur fjord. A ferry runs from Stykkishólmur across the water past the historic island of Flatey to the North West Fjord region.

The town has quite a few facilities for tourists, including a craft shop, café and restaurant. The district museum is located in the Norwegian house, while the space-age looking church on the hill occasionally presents concerts open to the public. Nature-watching excursions, offered by Seatours (🌐 www.seatours.is) take visitors

---

● *Stykkishólmur is a small but charming town in a dramatic setting*

out for trips on the Breidalfjördur fjord. Nearby, horse riding is available, and there's even a nine-hole golf course close to the Hotel Stykkishólmur.

CULTURE

Budir Church

Off a dirt road towards the sea, just past the Hotel Budir, is the charming Budir Church. Although some sort of religious edifice has been here since the early 18th century, this wooden building was built in 1847. Even though it's small, the church is still frequently used, often by couples wanting to get married in such a beautiful spot. ❷ Heading west, turn south off route 574 on to an ungraded road (signposted Budir), about 0.5 km (0.3 miles) after the junction with route 54.

Hellnar Church

Another of the small churches, this 1945 construction is notable for its incredible location, just beneath Snæfellsjökull. The building is a good point of reference on the Arnarstapi to Hellnar coastal walk. ❷ just north of the centre of the village.

Norwegian House (Norska husid) Folk Museum

Situated within a large Norwegian-style wooden building, the museum describes Stykkishólmur's local history.
❷ Hafnargata 5, Stykkishólmur ❶ 438 1640 ❸ Daily 11.00–17.00 June–Aug (Sept–May by arrangement).

The Old Warehouse (Gamla Pakkhúsid)

Olafsvik's past is portrayed in photographs and exhibits located in this 19th-century timber warehouse. Not surprisingly for such an important commercial port, the story of the area's fishing is featured. ② Gamla pakkhúsid, Ólafsvík. ❶ 436 1543.

Stykkishólmur Church

Prominently placed on a hill overlooking the sea, this modern-looking church also presents concerts every fortnight during the summer. Visitors are actively encouraged to attend.
② Borg, Stykkishólmur ❶ 438 1560.

RETAIL THERAPY

Most shops are in the larger villages, although service stations usually include small outlets that sell basics, together with a full range of fuels.

Service Stations (Bensínstod)
Arnarbær ② Arnarstapa ❶ 435 6783
Esso ② Adalgata 25 IS-340 Stykkishólmur ❶ 438 1254
Söluskáli OK Fast food ② Olafsbraut, Olafsvik ❶ 436 1012

Olafsvik
Apothek Olafsvikur Olafsvik's pharmacy has most of the supplies usually found at a chemist. ② Olafsbraut 24, Olafsvik ❶ 436 1261.

Blómaverk Even in Iceland, flowers are regular gifts. ② Olafsbraut 24, Olafsvik ❶ 436 1688.

Kasinn Edible necessities can be purchased at this small supermarket. ② Olafsbraut 55 ❶ 436 1500.

Stykkishólmur

Gallerí Lára Local craftsperson Lara Gunnarsdottir presents her work in this small venue. 🅐 Adalgata 13, Stykkisholmur 🅣 438 1617 🅦 frontpage.simnet.is/smavinir/lara.htm

Verslun Gissurar Tryggvasonar Head to where local people go and buy groceries at this supermarket. 🅐 Adalgata 25 IS-340 Stykkisholmur.

TAKING A BREAK

Braudgerdarhus Stykkisholms The town bakery provides snacks and goodies for a quick rest from all the activity 🅐 Nesvegur 1, Stykkisholmur.

Grillskálinn Even the provinces have fast food, which can be pretty handy at times 🅐 Ólafsbraut 19, Ólafsvík 🅣 436 1392.

Snjófell Within a traditional Icelandic turf house, this café serving light snacks is convenient for exploring both Snæfellsjökull and the Arnarstapi-Hellnar walk. 🅐 Arnarstapi 🅣 435 6783 🅦 www.snjofell.is

TAKING A DIP

Swimming enthusiasts can wallow in their passion under the shadow of the mystic mountain.

Budir Swimming Pool 🅐 750 Faskrudsfjordur, nr Budir 🅣 475 1214
Olafsvik Swimming Pool 🅐 355 Olafsvik 🅣 436 1199
Stykkishólmur Swimming Pool 🅐 340 Stykkisholmur 🅣 438 1272

⬤ *Some of the rooms in Hotel Budir offer great views of Snæfellsbær*

AFTER DARK

Outside of the big cities, the nightlife is pretty quiet.

Fimm fiskar £ Fish and pizza in a corrugated iron building in town.
ⓐ 340 Stykkishólmur ⓣ 438 1600

Hotel Budir £££ The excellent Hotel Budir provides superb gourmet
cuisine – at top-class prices. ⓐ 356 Snæfellsbær ⓣ 435 6700
ⓦ www.budir.is

ACCOMMODATION

Olafsvik Guesthouse £ Right in the centre of town, this guesthouse offers double, triple and 'quadro' rooms, as well as sleeping bag accommodation. Meals and excursions are also available.
🅐 Olafsbraut 19 IS-355 Olafsvik ☎ 436 1300 🆆 www.randburg.com/is/gistiolafs/index.asp

Stykkishólmur Hostel £ Warm accommodation is offered year round in this comfortable hostel, situated in one of the oldest houses in town. 🅐 Höfdagata 1, 340 Stykkishólmur ☎ 438 1095.

ECO Guesthouse-Brekkubær ££ At the edge of the National Park, this guesthouse adheres to the values of sustainable tourism.
🅐 Hellnar, 356 Snæfellsbær ☎ 435 6820
🆆 www.randburg.is/is/hellnar/brekkubaer.html

Hotel Budir £££ In a wonderful location by a lava field next to the sea, Snæfellsjökull is visible from most of the rooms. One of the best hotels in Iceland. 🅐 356 Snæfellsbær ☎ 435 6700 🆆 www.budir.is

Camping
Snjófell The little village has a large campsite equipped with toilet and shower blocks. 🅐 Arnarstapi ☎ 435 6783 🆆 www.snjofell.is

Tjaldstædid Stykkishólmur In the vicinity, the campsite is pleasantly located, close to the town's attractions. 🅐 IS-340 Stykkishólmur ☎ 438 1136.

◗ *Keflavík has all the facilities you would expect of a modern airport*

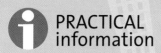

PRACTICAL
information

Directory

GETTING THERE

As Iceland is an island in the North Atlantic, the only ways of getting there are by air and sea.

By air

From the UK, three scheduled airlines fly to Reykjavik all year round: British Airways (Ⓦ www.britishairways.com), Icelandair (Ⓦ www.icelandair.co.uk) and the low-cost Iceland Express (Ⓦ www.icelandexpress.com). Icelandair has regular flights from various airports on both coasts of the United States as well as several cities in Europe. The airline also offers stopover packages in Reykjavik on transatlantic routes. Iceland Express includes some departure airports in Scandinavia and Germany.

During the summer, other airlines and charter operators ply the route, often in conjunction with package tours.

By boat

The Smyril Line (Ⓦ www.smyril.co.uk) is the only regularly scheduled ferry that operates all year. It runs between Norway and Denmark, to the Shetland Islands and the Faeroe Islands, before arriving at the eastern Iceland port of Seyddisfjörddur. During the summer, various cruise lines include a stopover in Reykjavik as part of their Arctic routes.

Package deals

Travel agents offer short trips, although there are several companies that arrange trips online. Arctic Experience/Discover the World (Ⓦ www.arctic-experience.co.uk) is one of the most experienced

⬤ *Your last glimpse of Reykjavik will probably be something like this*

operators in this region and can offer a range of options. Both
Icelandair (ⓦ www.icelandair.co.uk) and Iceland Express
(ⓦ www.icelandexpress.com) offer package breaks, although only
the former does them from the USA (ⓦ www.icelandair.com).

ENTRY FORMALITIES

Visa requirements

Visas are not required for passport holders from Australia, Canada,
New Zealand, Republic of Ireland, United Kingdom and United
States. South African citizens must obtain visas before arrival.

As a participant in the Schengen agreement, travellers from

other countries within the group do not, in principal, need to show documents. However, it is always advisable to travel with a passport or identity card.

Customs

There are no customs controls for visitors, providing they are carrying items for their own use, with the exception of the following:

Food The import of up to 3 kg of food is allowed, as long as the value is not more than £120.00.

Alcoholic beverages Travellers can import duty-free alcoholic beverages as follows: 1 litre spirits and 1 litre wine or 1 litre spirits and 6 litres beer or 1 litre wine and 6 litres beer or 2.25 litres of wine. The minimum age for bringing alcoholic beverages into Iceland is 20 years.

Tobacco 200 cigarettes or 250 g of other tobacco products. The minimum age for bringing tobacco into Iceland is 18 years.

Angling gear, riding gear and clothing which has been used outside Iceland, including gloves, boots and waders, may be brought into the country if it has been disinfected according to valid regulations. A certificate of disinfection, issued by an authorised veterinary officer, will be acceptable if presented to customs. If such a certificate is not presented, the gear has to be disinfected at the possessor's own cost on arrival.

For more information, check Ⓦ www.tollur.is

MONEY

Icelandic banknotes and coins are called Kronur. The usual notation for Icelandic currency is ISK or Kr. Notes are in the following denominations: 500, 1000, 2000 and 5000; while coins are in values

TAX-FREE SHOPPING

Iceland participates in a tax-free scheme and offers a refund of up to 15 per cent for tourists off a minimum purchase of 4000Kr. (around £35.00). After the completion of all purchases, go to the tourist office and claim the refund. The tax will be refunded in cash, but a credit card will be requested for security. If the relevant forms are not dropped off at the departure point (in most cases Keflavik airport), then the refund will be charged to the credit card.

of 1, 10, 50 and 100. It is advisable to change currency within the country, and change back before leaving, as foreign banks do not often deal with Kronur.

Generally, though, large amounts of cash are unnecessary, as credit cards can be used for almost any amount, even relatively small ones. Icelanders charge virtually everything. AMEX, Mastercard and Visa are common and readily accepted.

There are ATM machines in every town, and they accept Visa and Mastercard, as well as Cirrus and Maestro. Traveller's cheques are becoming less common, but can be changed at any bank.

HEALTH, SAFETY & CRIME

Iceland is one of the cleanest and safest countries in Europe, if not, indeed, the world. Fresh, running water is one of the nation's most important assets, and it's fine to drink it from almost any source, including taps. Bottled water is available, but it usually comes from the same place as the domestic supply.

In summer, insects can be a problem – Lake Myvatn means

'midge lake'. Although the bugs carry no diseases and are not dangerous, they can be very annoying. Taking along a decent insect repellent is recommended.

Temperatures can drop dramatically throughout the year, and it's a good idea to carry enough clothing to keep warm and waterproof, even during the summer. For weather information, see Ⓦ www.vedur.is or ⓣ 902 0600 44 for the forecast in English.

Decent hiking boots are essential if any kind of walking activity is planned. Break in the boots beforehand to prevent blisters, although make sure enough bandaids/plasters are on hand or on foot.

Pharmacies are called *Apoték* and are clearly named as such. They are open during business hours, with some continuing into the night. Most of Iceland's towns have at least one of them.

Iceland's medical facilities are excellent, but visitors should have either their EHIC card or adequate medical insurance. UK travellers are eligible for medical treatment under EU reciprocal health schemes, as long as they are in possession of a European Health Insurance Card.

It is very safe to walk along Iceland's streets even at night, particularly in Reykjavik on weekends, when the parties go on till the morning. However, it is always advisable to act sensibly, especially when the clubs close and drunken partygoers decide to head home. Even though it is very unusual, crime can happen, and it's best be cautious and ensure valuables are not within easy reach. Policemen are around, although not highly visible. They appear at street events or occasions when crowds gather, but they remain fairly low-key, and are pretty much seen only when potentially needed.

◀ *With a low crime rate, police in Reyjavik are not always as visible as this*

TRAVEL INSURANCE

However you book your city break, it is important to take out adequate personal travel insurance for the trip. For peace of mind the policy should give cover for medical expenses, loss, theft, repatriation, personal liability and cancellation expenses. If you are hiring a vehicle you should also check that you are appropriately insured and make sure that you take relevant insurance documents and your driving licence with you.

OPENING HOURS

Banking hours are Mon–Fri 09.15–16.00. At Keflavik Airport, the Landsbanki Islands (The Iceland National Bank) and the Change Group, located in the Transit Hall, are open daily 24 hours. Post offices are usually open Mon–Fri 08.30–16.30, although the one at Grensavegur 9 is also open on Sat 10.00–14.00.

Shopping hours are normally Mon–Fri 09.00–18.00, and Sat 10.00–13.00/14.00/15.00 or even 16.00, the closing time depending on the individual store. Supermarkets are open seven days a week, until 23.00.

Due to the country's location at such a northerly latitude, the amount of daylight varies dramatically between winter and summer and many organisations' business hours change accordingly. Standard opening times can often change depending on the time of year. Office hours are 09.00–17.00, although in summer these times are put forward an hour, from 08.00–16.00.

Hours vary from museum to museum; some are closed on Monday and others do not even open outside the summer. It's best to check the individual places beforehand.

TOILETS

There are public toilets throughout central Reykjavik, and they are clearly marked WC. Some appear in the new Euro-style, looking like large circular advertising displays. They are coin-operated, so make sure to have a few low-denomination Kronur on hand.

All restaurants and most coffee shops have public toilets. The locals don't mind outsiders visiting, although sometimes the number of cubicles are few, and the wait considerable. Discretion is advised!

Both the international and domestic airports are well supplied with public facilities.

CHILDREN

Children are very visible in Reykjavik, with parents taking them along whenever they can. It's not unusual to see a child's area in coffee houses (including Kaffitár ❷ Bankastræti 8), which provides entertainment for the young, while their parents imbibe their caffeine. Festivals always have events for children, and even the marathon has a special 3 km event especially for them.

Lots of activities that are entertaining for adults are also fun for smaller folk. Some that are especially for kids include the following:

- **Arbærsafn** This outdoor museum village is a good way to make the past interesting for young people. There is also a petting zoo, where children can get to know chickens, goats, sheep and Icelandic horses (see page 95).

- **Reykjavik Park and Zoo** The Zoo's speciality is Icelandic animals, while the Family Park has rides and activities. For older children there's Science World – a touchy-feely museum whose focus is on science and new technologies (see page 90).

- **Swimming pools** Reykjavik has several heated swimming pools that are open all year. Laugardalurslaug, with its waterslides and beachballs, is especially fun for kids. ⓐ Laugardalur ⓣ 553 4039 ⓛ Mon–Fri 06.50–21.30, Sat–Sun 08.00–20.00 (or see Taking a Dip, page 102).

⬇ The city's central duck pond is an impressive sight whatever your age

- **Tjörnin** The City Pond, right in the heart of town, has an almost constant supply of ducks, geese, swans and passing-through migratory birds. Join the other children – and their parents – in feeding them with the leftovers from breakfast (see page 75).

COMMUNICATIONS

Phones

Iceland's public phones come in three different varieties: credit, coin-operated, and pre-paid card. Pre-paid cards can be purchased at post offices and service stations around the country. Most people use mobile telephones, and foreign GSM systems work within the country. Alternatively, GSM phones may be rented from Iceland Telecom ⓐ Armulí 27, Reykjavik.

To make an international call from Iceland, dial 00, then the country code, the area or city code and then the number. For assistance ❶ 115, or for foreign information ❶ 114.

When dialing within the country, the Iceland prefix (354) can be dropped, and only the seven-digit number needs to be used. Note that the Icelandic telephone directory lists entrants alphabetically by their first, rather than their family, names.

To dial Iceland from abroad, dial the international access (00 from the UK, 011 from the USA), then 354, then the seven-digit number.

Post

There are post offices in many of Iceland's towns, and six within Reykjavik. Stamps are also available at most places where postcards are sold. Prices vary, depending on the destinations, with up to 20 grams domestic costing ISK 45, within Europe ISK 65, and outside Europe ISK 90. Post boxes are red, marked 'Pósturinn' in yellow letters.

Being halfway between Europe and North America, mail goes quickly between the continents, with, for example, a letter to the UK taking about three days to arrive. For further information, check out Ⓦ www.postur.is.

Internet

With computer usage one of the highest, per capita, in the world, the Internet is a way of life in Iceland. Most information is given alternatively as a website and it's possible to find out just about anything online. There are several internet cafés in town and some coffee houses have free wireless connection. Reykjavik Travel Service, (Ⓐ Laekjargata 2) also has access.

The Tourist Information Centre at (Ⓐ Adalstræti 2) is a convenient location to pick up messages, and the purchase of the Reykjavik Tourist Card entitles the owner to free web usage here.

ELECTRICITY

Electricity here works on the same system as the rest of Western Europe, with 220 volts (AC) and 50 hertz. The standard two-pin round-ended adapters are required for UK and USA electrical items.

TRAVELLERS WITH DISABILITIES

Although not totally equipped for the visitors with disabilities, Iceland is reasonably good at providing facilities, especially with prior notice. Many hotels and some of the larger department stores are wheelchair accessible, although most places recommend travelling with an able-bodied companion. All international flights and costal ferries are able to accommodate the disabled.

For more information regarding the Association of the Disabled in Iceland, as well as those places which are wheelchair friendly,

contact **Sjálfsbjörg** ⓐ Hátún 12, 105 Reykjavik ❶ 550 0300
🅦 www.sjalfsbjorg.is 🄻 Mon–Fri 08.45–12,00, 13.00–16.15.

TOURIST INFORMATION
Iceland Tourist Board ⓐ Lækjargata 3, Gimli 101 Reykjavik ❶ 535 5500
🅦 www.icetourist.is

Tourist Information Centre Reykjavik Complete ⓐ Adalstræti 2 101
Reykjavík ❶ 590 1500 🅦 www.visitreykjavik.is

Keflavík Airport – Leifsstöd Tourist Information Centre ⓐ Leifsstö,
235 Keflavík ❶ 425 0330 🅦 www.reykjanes.is. For international
correspondence, ⒠ rtb@rnb.is

Reykjanes Peninsula Tourist Information Centre ⓐ Kjarninn,
Hafnargata 230, Keflavík ❶ 421 5155 🅦 www.reykjanes.is

North-Iceland Tourist Information Centre ⓐ Hafnarstræti 82, 600
Akureyri ❶ 462 7733 ❶ 461 1817 🅦 www.eyjafjordur.is

FURTHER READING
The Icelandic Sagas, e.g. *Njall's Saga*
Dip into the Norse medieval world, and gain some understanding of
an integral part of Icelandic culture, by reading these 12–14th-
century stories that are part history, part adventure.
The Works of Halldor Laxness
Writing in his own language, the home-grown Nobel Laureate
wrote several books based on Icelanders themselves and is
considered one of the greatest European novelists of the 20th
century. His works are available in translated editions.

Useful phrases

Although English is spoken widely in Iceland, these words and phrases may come in handy. Note that r is often pronounced emphatically, shown as rr in the pronunciation guide.

English	Icelandic	Approx. pronunciation
BASICS		
Yes	Já	Yow
No	Nei	Nay
Please	Gjördu svo vel	Gyerthoo svo vehl
Thank you	Takk fyrir	Tahk firrirr
Hello	Halló	Hahlo
Goodbye	Bless	Blehss
Excuse me	Afsakid	Ahfsahkith
Sorry	Mér thykir thad leitt	Myehrr thikirr thahth leyt
That's okay	Allt í lagi	Ahlt ee layi
To	Til	Til
From	Frá	Frrow
Do you speak English?	Talar thú ensku?	Tahlahrr thoo ehnsker?
Good morning	Godan daginn	Gohthahn dayin
Good afternoon	Godan daginn	Gohthahn dayin
Good evening	Gott kvöld	Khot kverld
Goodnight	Goda nótt	Khoh-thah noht
My name is ...	Ég heiti ...	Yehkh heyti ...

DAYS & TIMES		
Monday	Mánudagur	Mowner-dahkher
Tuesday	Thridjudagur	Thrrith-yer-dahkherr
Wednesday	Midvikudagur	Mithviker-dahkherr
Thursday	Fimmtudagur	Fimter-dahkherr
Friday	Föstudagur	Ferster-dahkherr
Saturday	Laugardagur	Le-erkh-ah-dahkherr
Sunday	Sunnudagur	Sern-er-dahkherr
Morning	Morgunn	Morrgern
Afternoon	Eftir hádegi	Ehfdirr howdayi
Night	Noht	Nótt
Yesterday	I gær	Ee gyehr
Today	Hoy	Ee dahkh

English	Icelandic	Approx. pronunciation
Tomorrow	Á morgun	Ow morrgern
What time is it?	Hvad er klukkan?	Kvahth ehrr klerkahn?
It is ...	Hún er ...	Hoon ehrr ...
09.00	Níu fyrir hádegi	Nee-er firrirr howdayi
Midday	Hádegi	Howdayi
Midnight	Midnætti	Mithnehti

NUMBERS

English	Icelandic	Pronunciation
One	Einn	Aydn
Two	Tveir	Tvehrr
Three	Thrír	Thrreer
Four	Fjórir	Fyohrrrirr
Five	Fimm	Fim
Six	Sex	Sehx
Seven	Sjö	Syer
Eight	Átta	Owtdah
Nine	Níu	Nee-er
Ten	Tíu	Tee-er
Twenty	Tuttugu	Terterkher
Fifty	Fimmtíu	Fimtee-er
One hundred	Eitt hundrad	Eht herndrahth
One thousand	Eitt thúsund	Eht thoosernd

MONEY

English	Icelandic	Pronunciation
I would like to change these traveller's cheques/this currency	Ég tharf ad skipta ferdatékkum/peningum	Yehkh tharrf ahth skifdah fehrrthah-tyehkerm/ pehninkherm
What's the exchange rate?	Hvert er gengid?	Kvehrrt ehrr gehngith?
Credit card	Greidslukort	Grehth-sler-korrt

SIGNS & NOTICES

English	Icelandic
Airport	Fluhvalla
Smoking/ non-smoking	Reykingar/Reykingar bannadar
Toilets	Snyrting
Ladies/Gentlemen	Konur/Karlar
Subway	Opid/Lokad

155

Emergencies

EMERGENCY NUMBERS

Police ℹ 112
Emergency (24 hours) ℹ 551 1166
Information ℹ 569 9020.
Ambulance ℹ 112
Fire ℹ 112
Doctor (in emergency, Reykjavík area, 24 hours) ℹ 1770
Dentist (in emergency, the Reykjavík area) ℹ 575 0505 🕓 Sat–Sun 11.00–13. 00

HEALTH

Doctors and dentists are listed in the phone book. Alternatively, ask at your hotel or local tourist office. All medical practitioners in the country speak English. If the condition is urgent, but an ambulance is not required, go to the Emergency Room (*Slysadelid*) at the National University Hospital. 📍 Fossvogur ℹ 543 2000.

Emergency Pharmacies (*Apoték*)
There are two pharmacies in Reykjavik that are open 08.00–24.00:
Lyf og heilsa 📍 Haaleitisbraut 68 ℹ 581 2101
Lyfja 📍 Lagmuli 5 108 Reykjavik ℹ 533 2300

LOST PROPERTY

The main office for lost and found articles is at this police station.
📍 Borgartun 33. ℹ 569 9018 🕓 Mon–Fri 10.00–12.00, 14.00–16.00

CONSULATES & EMBASSIES

Australia Embassy (in Denmark) @ Dampfærgevej 26 2100 Copenhagen, Denmark 📞 7026 3676 🕐 Mon–Thur 08.30–16.30, Fri 08.30-16.00.

Canada Embassy @ Túngata 14 101 Reykjavík 📞 575 6500.

Republic of Ireland Embassy (Denmark) @ Østbanegade 21 2100 Copenhagen Denmark 📞 3542 3233 🕐 Mon–Fri 10.00–12.30,14.30–16.30.

South Africa Embassy @ Drammensveien 88 C 0271 Oslo, Norway 📞 2327 3220 🕐 Mon–Fri 08.00–16.00 Consular Section 📞 2327 3220 🕐 Mon–Fri 09.00-13.00.

UK Embassy @ Laufásvegur 31, 101 Reykjavík 📞 550 5100 🕐 Mon–Fri 08.30–12.00.

USA Embassy @ Laufásvegur 21 101 Reykjavík 📞 562 9100 🕐 Mon–Fri 08.00–12.30, 13.30–17.00. Consular Section: 📞 562 9100.

EMERGENCY PHRASES

Help! Hjálp! *Hyowlp!*

Call an ambulance/a doctor/the police!
Náid í sjúkrabíl/lekni/lögregluna!
Now-ith ee syookrahbeel/lehkni/lerg-rrehglernah!

Can you help me please?
Gætir thú hjálpad mér?
Gyehtirr thoo hyowlpahth myehrr?

INDEX

The publishers would like to thank Ethel Davies for supplying her copyright photographs for this book.

Copy editor: Deborah Parker
Proofreader: Jan McCann

Send your thoughts to
books@thomascook.com

- **Found a great bar, club, shop or must-see sight that we don't feature?**

- **Like to tip us off about any information that needs a little updating?**

- **Want to tell us what you love about this handy little guidebook and more importantly how we can make it even handier?**

Then here's your chance to tell all! Send us ideas, discoveries and recommendations today and then look out for your valuable input in the next edition of this title. As an extra 'thank you' from Thomas Cook Publishing, you'll be automatically entered into our exciting monthly prize draw.

Email the above address (stating the title) or write to:
CitySpots Project Editor, Thomas Cook Publishing, PO Box 227, Unit 15/16, Coningsby Road, Peterborough PE3 8SB, UK.